10 THOUGHTS TO PONDER

10
THOUGHTS
TO
PONDER

Book 1

FRANK BALL

10 Thoughts to Ponder — Book 1
A Buffet for the Inquisitive Mind
By Frank Ball

First Printing

Roaring Lambs Publishing
17110 Dallas Pkwy Ste 260
Dallas, TX 75248

Phone: 972.380.0123
Email: info@RoaringLambs.org
FBall@RoaringLambs.org

RoaringLambs.org
FrankBall.org

Introduction

People ask where I get so many interesting thoughts. If you think God is my source, then give him credit, not me. Please don't think he's responsible for my crazy statements or stupid ideas. I'll take the blame for those.

On the other hand, I often find that my wrong perceptions can lead to a better understanding of what is right. Or a statement that seemed a bit out-of-focus can help me see reality more clearly. So perhaps all ten random thoughts on the page can energize your faith, bring you a little closer to God, and amplify your personal stories of his greatness.

The *10 Thoughts to Ponder* book series naturally grew from more than thirty years of asking questions, pondering possibilities, and paying enough attention to write my insights each day so I could remember and grow in God's knowledge and wisdom. Now, I'm delighted to share whatever thoughts might help others thrive in this crazy, mixed-up world.

If a statement resonates with you, I pray that the Lord is speaking to your heart and I'm merely one means for his thoughts to become yours. Give him the praise, and I'll accept honorable mention.

— Frank Ball

Quest for Truth

Confucius was a philosopher in ancient China, sometimes regarded as "lord" and "master" because of his wisdom. I think he was bothered that so many men of his time didn't know who they were, where they were headed, or how they would get there.

Some people listened and were helped by his truth. Those who didn't like what he said went their own way.

> Pilate said, "Are you a king, then?"
> Jesus said, "Yes, you could say that. For that reason, I was born. I came into this world to testify to the truth. Everyone who wants the truth hears my voice."
> "What is truth?" Pilate said.
> — John 18:37–38

Ten Thoughts to Ponder
1. What we value most is what we will focus our lives upon.
2. Helping others is the greatest of all goals.
3. Communication problems are resolved through entirely open and honest communication with the Lord.
4. An itch can be captivating if not scratched.
5. God speaks in a whisper so people don't have to listen if they don't want to.
6. We might think having our own way is better, but having God's way is always best.
7. Without the Holy Spirit at work, social networks aren't worth much.
8. HOLY means Having Our Lord's Yearning.
9. Waiting upon the Lord means taking the next right step without knowing what future steps will be.
10. To be energized by the Spirit, we must be plugged-in.

Questions for Further Thought

- How much did Pilate know about Jesus?
- What kind of evidence is needed to be sure our truth is really true?

Genius at Work

Einstein amazed intelligent people with his theories, especially when they found those theories to be fact. Since then, physicists have discovered much more, yet the more we learn, the more we're aware of how much we don't know.

When Jesus walked on Earth, he didn't know *everything*. He's the perfect example of who we can be as we walk with God. Like Jesus, we can know by the Spirit whatever we need to know to fulfill his purpose for our lives.

> *The Lord says, "I don't think the way you think, and my methods are different from yours. As the stars are so distant from Earth, so are my thoughts and methods far above yours."*
> — Isaiah 55:8–9

Ten Thoughts to Ponder

1. The attic of our brain is loaded with information and ideas we don't need—until we need them.
2. We are easily enslaved by what we are taught.
3. Society will squelch non-compliant thinking.
4. We answer the phone because we think we have to—until we decide we don't want to.
5. Clichés kill creative thinking.
6. In a black-and-white world, color is unimaginable.
7. Many students have full backpacks and empty minds.
8. The question is more important than the answer, because it opens the mind to possibilities.
9. I have nothing more important to do than listen to the Lord.
10. If I really want to do something, I won't allow obstacles to hold me back.

Questions for Further Thought

- Suppose the Lord were to ask, "What did you learn yesterday?" Surely you learned something as you walked with him. How would you answer?
- What can we do to see the invisible hand of God at work?

Great BHAG

I've been told in seminars that my success depends on BHAG, pronounced bee-hag: a Big Hairy Audacious Goal. In other words, I must plan my work and work my plan. Dream big and never give up. When I consider the millions of businesses and individuals declaring bankruptcy each year, I'm thinking we might need a different BHAG.

Perhaps we should define our BHAG as Become Hungry After God so his plan becomes our plan. We don't have to dream big, because God's way is better than anything we can imagine. Then, our success strategy only requires following his guidance one step at a time.

As Isaiah wrote: Eye has not seen nor ear heard. No mind can even imagine the wonders that God has prepared for those who love him.
— *1 Corinthians 2:9*

Ten Thoughts to Ponder
1. The size of the mountain depends on our perspective.
2. How it can be used determines the difference between trash and treasure.
3. Without a desire to know, ignorance is bliss.
4. With God as my driving force, I still must drive.
5. A good sense of direction can only come from the Director, who knows all things.
6. When the Holy Spirit through Jesus Christ connects me to I AM, I can know who I am.
7. Where I'm going to be in five years is God's plan, not mine to make.
8. With God in control, listening and doing is more important than planning.
9. Making a choice eliminates other options.
10. The claim that there is nothing new under the sun limits the boundless creativity of God.

Questions for Further Thought

- What distinguishes ordinary dreams from spiritual dreams?
- How do God's ways differ from what people typically do?

Right Answers

In school, most kids didn't raise their hand when the teacher asked a question. If I didn't know the answer, I wanted to hide, because evidently I was supposed to know. If I knew, I said nothing, because my friends didn't like a know-it-all. If I wasn't sure, I feared the embarrassment of being wrong and wouldn't volunteer.

People sometimes defend their faith by saying, "I just believe the Bible." Actually, we mostly believe what we've been taught from our *interpretation* of Scripture. To know the right answer, we need the Holy Spirit to guide us.

When the Spirit of Truth comes, he will guide you into all truth. He will not speak on his own authority but will say only what he hears. He will reveal to you things to come.
— *John 16:13*

Ten Thoughts to Ponder

1. Being dead right is not the best goal.
2. With God, victory is achieved by total surrender to his will.
3. I can do all things only if I have put God in command.
4. I can look beyond the pain and suffering only when I'm certain it will work for good.
5. To embrace a lie as the truth, I must see the truth as a lie.
6. Burnout occurs, not from being overworked, but from losing focus on the value of the goal.
7. The *process* matters because it's the only means to reach the goal.
8. Sleep is wonderful, but not while you drive.
9. In asking God a question, I need to accept his response—or non-response.
10. Asking God, "What should I do?" is better than asking, "Why don't you?"

Questions for Further Thought

- Why did Pharisees and teachers of the Law think they knew the truth and wouldn't listen to Jesus, their greatest teacher?
- How can you be sure that what you believe is really true?

Progress

In slide-rule competition in 1960, I was ready to quit because my practice scores didn't show much improvement.

My teacher said, "Do you think you're getting worse?"

"Of course not." I'd never heard a more ridiculous question.

"Then stay at it," he said, "because you have to be getting better."

With that advice, I learned not to quit. I've known poor writers who succeeded because they refused to quit. I've also known great writers who failed because they quit.

When we're working to fulfill God's purpose, failure is never final. You may not see the progress, but it's there. It will all work together for good.

> *Never tire of doing good, for a harvest of blessing is certain if you never give up on God.*
> — *Galatians 6:9*

Ten Thoughts to Ponder

1. If I can be certain of God's purpose, I can find pleasure in the pain necessary to reach his valuable goal.
2. Achievement comes from finding pleasure in the process.
3. Frequent reminders make forgetting impossible.
4. With God's help, I can do more than try.
5. Transparency allows God's light to shine through us.
6. Grooves are good, unless they become ruts.
7. Procrastination is our enemy, because just a little progress today will benefit us for the rest of our lives.
8. Progress is knowing what to do next—and doing it.
9. The tough part of submitting to God is having to surrender my desires.
10. Knowing our thoughts and desires, God always hears our prayers, but he doesn't always choose to listen.

Questions for Further Thought

- What must we do to overcome a desire to quit?
- Under what conditions should we quit?

Going Up

My favorite tree in the back yard had a horizontal branch of just the right height for a teenage boy to leap, grab the branch like a chinning bar, and swing back and forth. I had done that so often, I could catch the branch with my eyes closed. One day, I ran around the house toward the tree, took a flying leap, and grabbed the branch. As I swung back and glanced down before dropping to the ground, I froze.

A three-foot snake lay coiled directly below, beneath my feet. I climbed up instead of going down. On that day, I promised to pay better attention to the evil that might pull me down.

Lord, protect me from the hands of cruel and violent people, who devise any way they can to make me stumble.
— *Psalm 140:4*

Ten Thoughts to Ponder
1. For signs to have value, they must be seen and followed.
2. To climb the mountain, I must cross valleys, being willing to go down so I can go up.
3. God's detours are important to avoid disasters.
4. When freshness is lost, I need refreshing.
5. A few well-chosen words can create a thousand pictures in different minds.
6. Persistence keeps going while Patience can wait.
7. God's anointing appoints people for work that they cannot possibly do on their own.
8. The difference between trash and treasure is the purpose for its collection.
9. When the distance is greater between us and God, hearing him becomes more difficult.
10. A little bit of excitement is like riding the crest of a wave without considering the potential for falling.

Questions for Further Thought

- How can we protect ourselves from dangers we don't see?
- What can we do to avoid being pulled down?

Wrong Way

I knew my first GPS wasn't very smart when it wanted me to take a road that led through a gated community. It didn't have the gate code, and neither did I. Now, my GPS is much better, pointing a way that seems wrong but is actually right, because it sees the traffic problems ahead, and I don't.

Am I sure that God can see what I don't see, that his direction is always right? If I know the right answer, why don't I always listen? Each time I mess up and God recalculates my best steps, I gain more confidence that his way is always better than mine.

Foolish people see their own way as right, but the wise listen to good advice.
— *Proverbs 12:15*

Ten Thoughts to Ponder

1. Wishing is a very weak force toward achievement.
2. To be led of the Spirit, I can't be the one taking the initiative.
3. Anxiety comes from knowing I'm not in control, and not being sure God is.
4. A claim has little value to the unbeliever when there is no proof.
5. My greatest need is God's guidance so I know what I need and not what I *think* I need.
6. People take the broad road to destruction because they don't see beyond their short-term pleasures.
7. I can't take a second step until after I've taken the first, so the *next* step is the most important in reaching my goal.
8. There is no sane argument that will cure insane beliefs.
9. Delight in the Lord causes my desires to be what he wants.
10. If I don't trust my GPS (God's Perfect Strategy), I won't follow its direction.

Questions for Further Thought

- How can we distinguish God's voice from our own imagination?
- When can we trust the advice of professional counselors?

No Respect

Completing university courses will reward graduates with diplomas and earn letters after their names, but what do they get for all that time and money? No respect, perhaps, because value is in the eye of the beholder. After graduating from high school, Rodney Dangerfield delivered groceries and sold newspapers for a living. He earned respect as a comedian by saying he never got any respect.

If Jesus, the greatest of all servants was disrespected, we should know we can't please everyone. The good we choose to do may not be well-received. But we can be sure that our love for God and our love for others will earn respect where it counts most.

The one we must please is God.

> *Don't forget to love others, helping those in need, for these are the sacrifices that please God.*
> *— Hebrews 13:16*

Ten Thoughts to Ponder
1. Prayer is birthed from our pain.
2. Our humble feelings of worthlessness allow God to make us worth more than we can imagine.
3. Watching the clock can be a waste of valuable time.
4. I am the Lord's when I have an insatiable appetite for what he wants.
5. I experience freedom when I am the Lord's prisoner.
6. The last impression is the lasting impression.
7. First impressions influence subsequent judgments.
8. Unconditional surrender to the Lord is our greatest victory.
9. God became like us in all ways except sin.
10. Unlike ancient cultures, today's readers don't need much description, because they've already seen most of it on TV.

Questions for Further Thought

- What can we do to increase our worth in God's eyes?
- How concerned should we be about what others think of us?

Diamond in the Rough

You can go to the Crater of Diamonds State Park in Arkansas, search for million-dollar gems, and take one home if you find one. I won't be visiting there anytime soon, because in my opinion, what I might find probably wouldn't exceed the cost for looking.

Jesus told about a man who found a buried treasure and sold everything to buy the field where it was. That's what Jesus did for us. He gave his life to have the field, not for all the dirt and rock, but for the chance to have us belong to him, diamonds in the rough.

> *I praise you, Lord, because of the awesome, unique way that you created me. You did wonderfully well, and my whole being knows and declares this truth.*
> — *Psalm 139:14*

Ten Thoughts to Ponder

1. When the process is right, achievement is inevitable and therefore of little concern.
2. Improving efficiency is crucial in raising the value of time spent.
3. There is no perfect timing for doing wrong.
4. To have their way, people must modify their definition of what they knew was good.
5. Actions speak louder than words, because they are the reality of experience.
6. Eliminating prepositional phrases intensifies the action.
7. God fills our world with color, unless we are colorblind.
8. God's help is according to *his* vision, not according to the way *I* envision it.
9. When God casts a shadow, it is filled with light.
10. Without cutting, grinding, and polishing, we are diamonds unable to radiate God's glory.

Questions for Further Thought

- If raw diamonds had feelings, how would they react to the pain of being cut and polished?
- Why are we so valuable that God would give his life for us?

Uncommon Sense

Working part-time in a wood shop, I was given the task of cutting quart-inch-thick two-inch-wide strips that would be used in building a church pew. Simple project. One after another, I cut strips in repetitive motion.

Ouch! Something bit me. No, not that. I'd run my thumb across the table saw blade. Common sense had led me to set the blade where I hadn't cut off the end of my thumb. But this experience gave me uncommon sense to never again come close to the blade.

As mature adults can chew tough meat, those who have been through a lot have their spiritual senses exercised to distinguish between good and evil.
— Hebrews 5:14

Ten Thoughts to Ponder
1. Spiritual strength is built from a healthy diet of God's word and exercise of his will.
2. Glorifying God means to recognize and express his value.
3. Imagining God is a great way to avoid actually knowing him.
4. If I don't know what I can't see, I can't measure the extent of my blindness.
5. Hearing is what our ears naturally do, but listening requires a conscious choice to engage our minds.
6. I could hear the Lord better if I didn't spend so much time talking, telling him what he already knows.
7. When I open the door to Jesus, I am welcoming him into his house.
8. I become God's prized possession when I surrender to him.
9. Home improvement is more important within ourselves than anywhere else.
10. Any improvement that can be made today is priceless when its value continues forever.

Questions for Further Thought

- Why don't some people have common sense?
- What might make it difficult to learn from our experiences?

Good Enough

At work, my boss said, "If you can't do the job, I'll find someone who can." I was doing my best. What more could I do but find another job where I would be good enough?

Jesus told about a man who didn't use his talent, because he thought he couldn't meet his boss's expectation. With God, we don't have to worry about that, because doing our best to please him is always good enough. He only wants our wholehearted effort and no more. *He's* the miracle worker who will use our small investment to produce amazing results.

> *Whatever you do for people, give your best effort to please the Lord, knowing that the greatest reward comes from serving him.*
> — *Colossians 3:23–24*

Ten Thoughts to Ponder
1. Jesus is the perfect example of who we are to become.
2. I must rely upon God for strength, or I cannot possibly do what he has for me to do.
3. One of God's most amazing gifts is our ability to communicate—to understand and to be understood.
4. If I am ever smart, it's because God gave me the smarts.
5. It is the nature of God to care for others more than he cares for himself, so clearly demonstrated by his death so we could live.
6. Eternity is an inconceivable amount of time.
7. Always do your best, and you won't have as many mistakes to fix.
8. Self-deception is the worst of all misdirection.
9. The greatest discoveries are truths revealed by the Holy Spirit.
10. Unbelief is blind sight.

Questions for Further Thought

- Why might pleasing people be more difficult than pleasing God?
- What should we do if we feel like we haven't pleased God?

Learning to Love

Since I was the firstborn in my family, I got all the attention from my parents, grandparents, aunts, and uncles. Then my baby sister came along, and I was no longer the center of the universe. I had a lot to learn about love.

God made us with a need to be loved, and he can fill that void like nobody on Earth can. But to enjoy the fullness of his love, we must love others as he loves us, which includes even our enemies.

If I predict the future, understand mysteries, and answer all questions—with such trust in God that mountains are moved—I am nothing without love for people.
— *1 Corinthians 13:2*

Ten Thoughts to Ponder

1. For everything to be enjoyable, I need to recognize the Lord in all things.
2. Prayer shows how much I care, but it may not convince God to give me what I want—unless it's what *he* wants.
3. The more we care, the more our thoughts are captured by what we care about.
4. God is the complete definition of love, which makes love impossible to completely define.
5. The love of God is caring enough to sacrifice everything he has to make me, the trash, like him, the treasure.
6. Extreme ignorance is not knowing and not knowing that I don't know.
7. A government by and for the people cannot be righteous when the people are unrighteous.
8. "Joy unspeakable" is an out-of-this-world feeling.
9. Anything I do independent from God can't be something I should be proud of.
10. Fools know but don't understand.

Questions for Further Thought

- How can God expect people to love their enemies?
- Are you anything like what your enemies think of you? Why?

Unbelievable Magic

Babies laugh in a game of peekaboo because Mommy is gone and then magically reappears.

At a trade show, I watched intensely from a foot away, but I never figured out how he could hold up an ace of hearts by the corner, turn the back to face me, and show me the card was not an ace but a jack of clubs.

God made a man out of dirt and a woman out of a man's rib. He caused the Red Sea to part, the water forming a wall on each side, so millions of Israelites with all their ox carts and livestock could cross on dry land.

Unexplainable magic is something we see with our own eyes. We know there's a cause, but we can't imagine how it's done.

Using dust from the ground, God created a man and breathed life into his nostrils, causing him to be a living being.
— *Genesis 2:7*

Ten Thoughts to Ponder
1. The excitement of embracing the truth comes from recognizing its value.
2. The things we cannot control have to be left to God, or we die in frustration.
3. God is the one boss we must please, because we can't please everyone.
4. Without the process, we wouldn't value the prize.
5. Eager anticipation is a lot more fun than anxiety.
6. I cannot imagine what I have not yet experienced.
7. There is a spiritual dimension to understanding that I don't understand.
8. To learn, I must admit that I didn't already know.
9. Traffic congestion is caused by so many people not being where they need to be.
10. I am fascinated by the fascinating way God does all things.

Questions for Further Thought
- Why did God make Adam in his image?
- Why did God use a rib and not dust to make Eve?

Talking to a Friend

If I could talk to my favorite teacher in eighth grade, I'd share my love for algebraic functions. I'd love to talk to my ninth-grade teacher to tell her she was wrong about my inability to write. I wish I could talk to Daddy about all that's happened since he left for Heaven.

Of all the friends I've gained and lost, I still have one friend I can talk to at any time, without fear of any consequence for being completely open and honest. God is always here to listen, for he understands me the best of all friends.

In desperation, I cried unto the Lord. From his heavenly dwelling place faraway, he heard my voice and listened to my plea for help. Since you know how much God cares, you can surrender all your worries to him.
— Psalm 18:6; 1 Peter 5:7

Ten Thoughts to Ponder
1. Without a little humor, life becomes rather boring.
2. With all the concerns I *shouldn't* have, I can miss the concerns I *should* have.
3. My actions can reach panic mode when they become matters of life and death.
4. Knowing has value only if we practice what we know.
5. Great stories torch the heart and leave it burning for a while.
6. Obstacles are the catalyst of conflict.
7. God's mission must drive my methods, or I'm manipulating him to get my way.
8. If the Lord isn't my source of excitement, then I am missing the most important resource.
9. Know the Lord, because he knows the thrill of life better than anyone else and is eager to share it.
10. Without progress, excitement about the future is difficult.

Questions for Further Thought

- What must we do to make God our friend and not an enemy?
- How can we be sure that God cares enough to listen to whatever we have to say?

Only Believe

I'm amazed at how easily I can believe a lie and at the same time, struggle to accept the truth. My parents said I was smart and could be the best at anything I wanted to be. Others said I was dumb and didn't have a chance. True or not, whatever I chose to believe would shape my actions.

Whatever greatness I could achieve wouldn't be worth anything without God. That presented a problem, because I'd never have the ability to do whatever he expected. Then I found out I was highly qualified because I was so weak and helpless, needing him.

> *God uses what the world regards as foolishness to embarrass those who think they are so smart. Through our weaknesses, he will do mighty things that confound those who hold positions of power.*
> — *1 Corinthians 1:27*

Ten Thoughts to Ponder

1. I have no choice when I tell myself I have no choice—and I believe it.
2. I won't pick up a penny if I don't think it is worth my effort.
3. To help the helpless, I need God's help.
4. If I love the Lord and desire whatever he wants, no matter the cost, then I have nothing to worry about.
5. If I want to know, I have no choice but to look.
6. My actions create circumstances, and circumstances create my reactions.
7. To avoid being late, I must be early.
8. Urgency can interrupt my urgency so much that I hardly notice what is important.
9. Little changes make big differences.
10. When urgencies become emergencies, patience is hard to find.

Questions for Further Thought

- How can we know that our beliefs are based on fact, not fantasy?
- In pursuit of what we believe God would have us do, what should we think about the obstacles we face?

Costly Choice

When I saw a neat jigsaw in the store, I asked Daddy if he would buy it for me, and I would pay him back. "Sure you can have it," he said, "as soon as you save enough from your seventy-five-cent allowance to pay for it." By the time I had saved that much, I didn't think the jigsaw was worth the cost.

To follow Christ, we must know it's worth the cost.

> *If you were going to build a tower, wouldn't you first sit down and calculate the cost? ... Likewise, if you are not ready to give up everything you have, you cannot be my disciple.*
> — *Luke 14:28, 33*

Ten Thoughts to Ponder

1. The corollary to Romans 8:28: "All things will work together for bad for those who love something other than the Lord or seek something other than what he wants."
2. Perfect timing is having exactly what we need at the time we need it. Not before. Not after.
3. We cannot be satisfied unless we can accept God's provision as enough for today and not worry about tomorrow.
4. Free will isn't without obligation.
5. After weighing the values and costs, we don't really have a choice but to do what we think is best.
6. Reactions are choices ignored.
7. Ignorance makes it impossible to know if I am making the best choice.
8. Because decisions are driven by my desire, I need God's help to want only whatever he wants.
9. Our free will says an omnipotent God can't force us to make a choice we don't want to make, but it could cost us our lives.
10. If I *think* I know, then as far as I know, I know.

Questions for Further Thought

- Why do people often max out their credit cards?
- When have you paid a lot for something, found out it wasn't worth it, and learned an important lesson?

Being Blessed

Mama made sure my diaper was changed and I was fed. For that reason, I'm sure the first word I learned to say was *Mama*. If I was anything like my three sons, my next words were *no* and *mine*.

I was born self-centered, only concerned about getting. Now that God is my provider, not Mama, I do well to understand that my blessings depend on my giving, not getting.

Give, and you will not have to worry about receiving. You will receive a full measure, packed down, shaken together, and spilling into your lap. The measure you give determines the measure you will receive.
— *Luke 6:38*

Ten Thoughts to Ponder

1. As long as I love the Lord and I'm striving to fulfill God's purpose for my life, I can be comfortable not knowing the future.
2. If I'm not looking, I'll miss seeing the good purpose God has for allowing my pain.
3. I wonder why I wonder and wonder and wonder. Suddenly the light dawns, and I don't have to wonder anymore.
4. The most important aspect of prayer is gaining confidence that God knows what he is doing.
5. Learning is finding a way to connect the dots when they have no numbers to show how they should come together.
6. We haven't learned until something changes in what we think.
7. The greatest challenge to learning is thinking I already know.
8. The process of getting there is more important than the prize, because there is no prize without the process.
9. Spiritual blessings of faith, hope, and love will not meet the world's standards for blessings.
10. People who think God doesn't know their thoughts should think again.

Questions for Further Thought

- How do God's blessings differ from what the world values?
- What kinds of giving does God respect most?

White Lies

As a youngster, I decided I wasn't smart enough to remember all the lies I would have to tell to cover for the first lie. Telling the truth was painful at first, but I soon found it refreshing and liberating because I didn't have to remember what I said before.

Nobody ever told a lie but what they thought they had something to gain. Therefore, all lies may appear *white* to the one telling them, but they are destructive. If Jesus never lied, why should we? Perhaps because our motives aren't what they ought to be. Ask for God's help to always *want* to do right. With pure motives, it's easier to admit the truth and avoid telling the lie when you've messed up.

Since you are no longer the person you used to be, always be truthful, avoiding all kinds of deception.
— *Colossians 3:9*

Ten Thoughts to Ponder

1. If I'm not looking, I'll miss seeing the gifts God has for me.
2. The greatest lesson to learn is how to learn.
3. When I say I'm smart, I've unwittingly shown my ignorance.
4. Faith unto righteousness is hearing God's voice, believing what he says, and acting upon that unseen reality.
5. Lying to others is possible only after you have lied to yourself.
6. Love becomes lust when getting is more important than giving.
7. What I do reveals whether what I say is really true.
8. Faith in God is not a weather forecast of percentage probability.
9. God has the only life insurance with a death benefit for the policy holder.
10. Life goes on, but exactly how it will go, I cannot know for sure, because I am not the one in control.

Questions for Further Thought

- Why does our culture so often expect people to lie?
- How can we sense when someone has lied to us?

Patient Persistence

Nobody ever had to learn how to be impatient. We're born with that ability, as infants crying to be fed immediately. Are we better as adults? Perhaps you've noticed how quickly drivers will pull over to the next lane, just to get one car length closer to the red light as they wait. If the front car doesn't immediately go on green, we hear honking.

Persistence says we aren't going to wait unnecessarily. Many things need to be handled right now.

As we walk with the Lord, we get to learn a very important lesson: some things are worth the wait, no matter how long it takes.

We can be thankful for delays that bring patience, because endurance is essential for receiving God's promise.
— *Hebrews 10:36*

Ten Thoughts to Ponder

1. Without death, there can be no resurrection.
2. Patience and persistence are fraternal twins.
3. The opposite of patience is unbelief.
4. Giving up what we want, for the sake of what we know is right, requires a clear understanding of value.
5. The smallest things can be of the greatest consequence.
6. Temptation is an opportunity to go the wrong way if we want.
7. Tests reveal whether we are less or more than who we thought we were.
8. Listening has no value when my thoughts, feelings, and actions don't change.
9. True riches come from huge investments in the Bank of Heaven.
10. Every day presents a new opportunity for me to surrender to the Lord what I want so I can have what *he* wants.

Questions for Further Thought

- What circumstance might have taught you that "haste makes waste"?
- How can we become more patient and considerate of others?

Supernatural Strength

I'm 5'10" and can jump a foot into the air. That's a far cry from being good enough to dunk a basketball. Without a ladder, such a dream will never happen.

Believing in a miracle has value only when the miracle worker makes his strength available to us. Peter walked on water, but not without the Lord's help. Since all things are possible with God, I can believe I will fly. But will it happen so I can look like Michael Jordan? Only if God decides to lift me up.

> *With your strength, God, I can break through the army's front lines and leap over the wall.*
> — *2 Samuel 22:30*

Ten Thoughts to Ponder
1. Strength without doing—that's like food left to spoil.
2. A tremendous amount of strength might be needed to let go so God can have his way.
3. Avoiding anger and turning the other cheek requires supernatural strength.
4. The first step toward my seeing better is understanding that I can't see very well.
5. When something is, but I say it shouldn't be, I am making an argument against reality.
6. My best agenda is to have one item at the top of my list for immediate focus. Ignore the rest until that one is finished.
7. As a ladder has only one top rung and one next rung, I can have only one ultimate goal that is reached by taking the next right step.
8. Learning without study is a result without purpose.
9. Without the truth, a lie cannot be recognized.
10. Information without purpose is meaningless filler.

Questions for Further Thought

- Why do people underestimate their abilities? Why might they think too highly of themselves?
- How great is the power of positive thinking?

Unequal Partnership

I once worked for a company owned by two brothers who were equal partners, one responsible for manufacturing, the other for sales. Corporate growth was stunted, because one brother's progressive idea was often vetoed by the other.

Wouldn't it be nice if we could have a partner who made no mistakes and supported us with every good idea and deny what wasn't? Who would that be? As God's partner, we can work with confidence knowing he will support what he knows is best.

> *If two people can't agree on the direction they should go, how can they walk together? Don't share goals with unbelievers.*
> — *Amos 3:3; 2 Corinthians 6:14*

Ten Thoughts to Ponder

1. Giving it all up to the Lord is much better than hanging on to something I can do nothing about.
2. Without common goals, partnership is a delusion.
3. We pray and nothing happens. We make that assumption when we can't see the hand of God at work.
4. Since God is easily touched by the feeling of our infirmities, he cannot ignore our prayers.
5. Patience requires waiting for the prompting of the Holy Spirit.
6. With the prompting of the Holy Spirit, patience doesn't have to wait any longer.
7. Patience waits for the *right* time, not the *perfect* time.
8. With high expectations for myself, I will react with impatience. But with high expectations for the Lord, I will react with patience.
9. The beauty of God's handiwork would take our breath away, if only we could see it.
10. Grace is "unmerited favor," yet people think they must do something to deserve God's favor and lessen their pain.

Questions for Further Thought

- What's the best approach when people don't agree?
- What can we do when we're not sure what God wants?

Fading Memory

People laugh when I say my memory is fine. Smiling, I say, "I can't remember *anything* I've forgotten." With a brilliant mind unlike any other, Jill Price lives a curse, having no ability to forget. She can't selectively remember the good times and forget the pain of her past.

The more we focus on faults, failures, and losses, the more we hurt ourselves. To forget, we need to focus on the positive events that brought us closer to the Lord. Then meditate upon the glorious future that God has planned for us.

Forget the past, because your history doesn't define your future.
"Look," the Lord says, "I'm doing something new. It's about to happen.
Can't you see it coming?
— Isaiah 43:18–19

Ten Thoughts to Ponder

1. The harder I try to forget my mistakes, the more vividly I remember.
2. I learn the most when I can embrace the reward of the pain as well as the pleasure.
3. If it weren't for our struggles, we wouldn't have a story to tell.
4. The beginning of something new is a crucial turning point that deserves special attention—to be sure it is taking us in the direction God wants us to go.
5. I at least need to be smart enough to know when I don't know.
6. I could explore the unknown if I knew where it was.
7. If I expect progress, I must overcome significant challenges.
8. With lofty goals and high expectations, we set ourselves up for disappointment and failure.
9. Without God's guidance, being determined is destructive.
10. For those who choose the broad road to destruction, everything works together for bad, not good.

Questions for Further Thought

- What are some good things you can be really excited about?
- How can you avoid negative influences that drag you down?

Believing in God

I used to believe the common saying, *Seeing is believing.* Not anymore. I'm amazed at how many people either can't or won't believe what they're seeing. Therefore, I'm more inclined to think the correct saying is, *Believing is seeing.*

Many people don't believe God exists. How is that possible? The apostle Paul says his creation makes it obvious. Every day in my biology class, I learned more about creation, proving God's existence. Maybe they don't believe, because they don't want to.

> *Jesus said, "Blessed are those who have not seen me, yet believe."*
> — *John 20:29*

Ten Thoughts to Ponder
1. With *spiritual* awareness, one can know yet not understand.
2. As long as God is guiding my steps, I don't have to know where I'm going.
3. I only have opinions. God knows.
4. Something is spectacular when we can see the fireworks.
5. If I think I can see, trusting God's guidance becomes more difficult.
6. Because it has no predictable pattern, reality is much more exciting than formality.
7. Anything counterfeited proves the existence and value of what is being counterfeited.
8. Without God's help, I am much too complex to understand myself, let alone anybody else.
9. A telescope and a microscope will show me reality beyond what I can see with the naked eye, but that won't get me close to the unlimited scope of reality that only God can see.
10. If God has no purpose in my actions, I have experienced a waste of energy and time.

Questions for Further Thought

- Why might people *not want* to believe in God?
- For what reasons might a person believe a god exists but be unwilling to believe in Jesus, God's Son?

Bullheaded

What's the difference between being bullheaded and being persistent? One is more dangerous than the other. *Persistent* Christians don't have to force their way like the bull in the china closet. They can be patient because they know the Lord, who makes a way when there doesn't seem to be one. I'm trying to be persistent, but not bullheaded.

Persistence says, "I will keep doing all I can to please the Lord, never giving up. Instead of pushing for my own way, I'll take one step at a time as he leads."

If the Lord is directing our steps, how can we be in a position to understand the whole journey?
— *Proverbs 20:24*

Ten Thoughts to Ponder
1. I don't have an ability that can be productive without God's support, which keeps me dependent upon him.
2. Sometimes I wish what I have been taught would be true, but I have a sense that it isn't actually true.
3. When I accept the way things are, I have a better chance of changing the way things are.
4. Believing God's miracle lets me do more than try.
5. Satan is the "father of lies" because of his ability to tell the truth in a deceptive way.
6. With faith, I can accept the way things are, knowing they won't stay that way.
7. My sight isn't good enough to see all the mountains that God moves.
8. With lots of prayer, I can learn to trust God's answers.
9. Persistence must see the benefit outweighing the cost.
10. I will give up as soon as I believe there is no hope.

Questions for Further Thought
- How far should we go in planning what we want to accomplish in the years ahead?
- How can we distinguish unnecessary delays and detours from God having a plan different from what we expect?

Perfect Image

I love the Rocky Mountain peaks, where the view takes my breath away. At night, I look up and see the Milky Way with its billions of glimmering stars and wonder how God created it all in just six of his days, perhaps over thirteen billion years of Earth days.

At home, my view is a computer screen with pictures that give me a feel for what exists beyond my limited world. I have no pictures of God? Or do I? If we'll study and visualize everything Jesus said and did, we have the perfect image.

> *Christ is the visible image of our God whom we otherwise could not see, who preceded all creation.*
> — *Colossians 1:15*

Ten Thoughts to Ponder
1. Half of eternity is as big as all eternity.
2. God is an unlimited resource who cannot be measured.
3. The smallest thing can be the greatest thing when God is in it.
4. When I am feeling insignificant, I allow myself to be unaware of God's significance in my life.
5. If the motives aren't right, then persistence is a liability, not an asset.
6. Frustration comes from assuming responsibility for an outcome without the ability to make it happen.
7. If I'm on the wrong side of the fence, the grass really is greener on the other side.
8. Appetite deserves careful consideration, because what looks good can be fatal.
9. With excellent hearing, I gain confidence that I might have the right words to say.
10. Pain and praise are like mixing oil and water, but it *can* be done.

Questions for Further Thought

- What characteristics of Jesus are most important for gaining a realistic perception of God?
- What aspect of God do you think are incomprehensible?

Feeling Our Pain

A poem in the late 1800s said we shouldn't judge a man unless we've walked in his moccasins. If God has never worn our shoes, we might find it difficult to believe God understands our problems and feels our pain. The Bible says he understands us, even knowing our thoughts, but what do we have beyond the words of a few writers?

Jesus had God for his father, making him divine, and his birth through the virgin Mary made him fully human. God in human flesh was so much in touch with our pain that he gave his life so we might be free from sin and live without pain.

> *Although Jesus was God, he did not act like he was better than everybody else. Instead of coming in royal attire, asking to be served, he worked as a lowly member of the servant class.*
> *— Philippians 2:6–8*

Ten Thoughts to Ponder

1. God's way is always the best way, because it is that way.
2. When everything is surrendered to the Lord, we don't have to suffer the pain of great loss.
3. Christians are not limited to this life, because they have all of eternity to work God's will.
4. Never underestimate small steps, because they will determine where you are going.
5. After doing all I know to do, I'm desperate for God's help to know what to do.
6. If I want true success, God is my best Mastermind resource.
7. If doing good made people righteous, then Jesus didn't have to die. He died because we must *be* good, not just *do* good.
8. I only have value when God uses me to fulfill his purpose.
9. My significance became significant when God changed me from nothing to something.
10. Without comparison, measuring value is impossible.

Questions for Further Thought

- How would you react if Jesus were to appear before you now?
- What does "access to God through Jesus Christ" mean?

No Worries

In grade school, I learned to worry. What if the teacher gave a pop quiz? Will anybody want to come to my birthday party? If my report card isn't perfect, how will my parents react? As an adult, I became much smarter. I listed potential problems that covered many pages of worries, beginning with: What if this insane culture gets even worse?

Now I'm learning that I don't have to worry about what I can't control. With God in control, I can dismiss most of those worries and focus my concern on what he would have me do right now.

Do not worry about tomorrow, for tomorrow will have its own worries. Today's problems are enough for today.
— *Matthew 6:34*

Ten Thoughts to Ponder
1. When I expect too much, I set myself up for disappointment.
2. The worst starvation in this world is from a lack of faith, not food.
3. The problem with ignorance is not knowing right from wrong.
4. The difference between plodding and racing is the perception of the goal and how to get there.
5. What we choose to do is somewhere between the way things are and the way we want them to be.
6. Because of all the years spent to get us here, this year will be the best ever.
7. Those who don't know the Lord are in the perfect position to think the future will be worse than the past.
8. Forever is an immeasurable length of time.
9. The problem with expectations is how they affect the future.
10. If I'm concerned about the future, I should be more concerned about today.

Questions for Further Thought

- Why do people worry about things they cannot control?
- What can you do right now that would reduce your reasons for worry?

I Am

Let's see …
    I am …
    I am who I am.
    I am who I think I am.
    I am who others think I am.
    I am who God knows I am.
    I am not capable of being someone else.
    I am not yet the person I would like to be—in God's image.
    I am capable of being a better me—but only with God's help.

> *I have learned to be content, no matter what the circumstances are.*
> *— Philippians 4:11*

Ten Thoughts to Ponder

1. With our limited knowledge, we deal with symptoms while only God can help us with the cause.
2. God doesn't watch the clock, because he has all the time he needs.
3. Through people, God accomplishes what neither he nor the people could do independently.
4. We change our desires by the conscious choice of delighting in the Lord, an act of free will that we can change but God cannot.
5. Our written words are important when they apply the talk to the walk.
6. When I think I know, I still don't know what I don't know.
7. God is an entirely different get-rich opportunity of eternal value.
8. People waste their lives on treasures with no lasting value.
9. Questions are essential to internalize external truth.
10. Disappointment comes from an inability to see enough progress.

Questions for Further Thought

- What can make us "comfortable in our own skin"?
- Why are cosmetics a multi-billion-dollar industry?

The Greatest Gift

On Christmas morning 1950, the last present I opened was a leather Bible with my name imprinted in gold letters. I never read it, but I carried it with me to church every Sunday, feeling very important.

The following Christmas, I got a comic book. Wow! I loved comic books. This one was 8½"x11" and ¾" thick, filled with Bible stories. I read it so many times, the cover wore out and came off.

Your Word is a lamp to keep my feet from stumbling, a light that shines before me to show the way you want me to go.
— Psalm 119:105

Ten Thoughts to Ponder

1. The most difficult part of time dedicated to hearing God's voice is not hearing anything.
2. My actions may not depend upon my comfort, but they must depend upon my conviction.
3. What God wants is what we need, so what we don't need is to tell God what we want.
4. God's needs justify the actions we don't understand when we don't get what we want.
5. What we think we know, even if we really do know, is just a fraction of what God knows.
6. All we have to do to experience God's miracles is to make ourselves part of what he wants to do.
7. A genuine expression of gratitude to God is impossible without recognizing his value.
8. Unexpressed gratitude is a diamond hidden from sight.
9. Moment by moment throughout the day, whatever I do is a matter of choice. I say I have no choice only because I've already decided what I must do.
10. What I want can cause me to ignore what would otherwise influence what I want.

Questions for Further Thought

- Why don't people spend more time studying Scripture?
- What can make the Bible easier to understand?

Dreaming

In a dream, Joseph saw the sun, moon, and eleven stars bow to him. If that dream was as vivid as the dreams that turned my life in an entirely different direction, I can understand why he had to tell others. His dreams certainly changed his life in ways he could never have anticipated.

His father, Jacob, also had a dream that changed his life.

> *As he dreamed, he saw a stairway from Earth to Heaven, and God's angels were going up and down the stairs. When Jacob woke up, he said, "Surely the Lord is in this place, and I didn't know."*
> — *Genesis 28:12, 16*

Ten Thoughts to Ponder

1. Dreaming is worthless roleplay unless it becomes reality.
2. God is grieved beyond description because he cannot force us to accept his priceless gift of salvation.
3. A closed mind can only be unlocked from the inside.
4. God's inaction is as much a miracle as his action.
5. Unlike me, God cannot act without knowledge, understanding, and purpose.
6. The word spectacular acquires greater meaning when we see more of God at work.
7. God's light shining through us is crucial to brighten our very dark world.
8. Our greatest opportunity is to take the next right step with the Lord.
9. Until we recognize the problem, we're in no position to appreciate the solution.
10. We don't always know what we want, let alone know what God knows we need.

Questions for Further Thought

- How can we avoid nightmares and enjoy only pleasant dreams?
- What distinguishes a dream from the Lord and a dream from our memories, activities, and concerns?

Easy Money

I must be the luckiest guy on Earth. Would you believe I received an email from a rich oilman who had billions of dollars to give away, and my name had been selected? An uncle I didn't know had died and left millions to his heirs. All I had to do was certify that my name matched his. For a thousand dollars, I could have owned a diamond mine in Africa. Many people are interested in such offers. I wasn't.

God's promise for eternal life and to walk with me through the hard times is the only amazing deal that I can trust with my life.

The Lord says, "You should seek treasure from me because my gold is 100 percent pure, of the highest value. Then you really will be rich."
— Revelation 3:18

Ten Thoughts to Ponder
1. Our worries should be limited to what God has for us today.
2. Experiencing all of God is a task that has no end.
3. My actions can't be right unless I have first heard the Lord and believe.
4. When God allowed evil, he created something that he is not capable of being.
5. Experiencing God's promises requires meeting his conditions.
6. An agreement has value only when all parties have an unwavering commitment to meet the conditions.
7. We get confused about God's promises because we don't understand the conditions.
8. People have the uncanny ability to lie to themselves—and believe it.
9. Negative influences aren't dangerous until people choose to embrace them.
10. The problem I imagine may be nothing more than a symptom that keeps me from recognizing the real problem.

Questions for Further Thought
- Why do people buy lottery tickets when they have a better chance of being struck by lightning on a clear day?
- How can you tell when a deal is too good to be true?

Did It My Way

When I was two, the milkman left quart bottles of whatever my mom wanted. "Three white, one chocolate," she said. The one chocolate was for me. The next week, I was out on the porch, waiting. I knew exactly what to tell the milkman when he arrived. "Three chocolate, one white," I said.

Slowly but surely after that, I had to learn that my way wasn't always the best way.

> *Obviously, those who want to make their own, independent decisions about what is best for them cannot please God.*
> — *Romans 8:8*

Ten Thoughts to Ponder

1. Being open and honest with people is impossible unless we have first learned to be open and honest with the Lord.
2. Wholehearted worship comes after our recognition of God's greatness has made our pain and suffering seem insignificant.
3. Godliness with contentment is great gain when we count our blessings and no longer see any need to count our losses.
4. The battle is lost as soon as we quit fighting.
5. There is no quitting as long as we see value in the effort.
6. Passion without progress is a waste of energy.
7. The only way I can expect God to give me what I want is to want what he wants.
8. All my life, God has supplied my needs. And that includes some pain and suffering and a few spankings.
9. Forgiving an offense won't meet God's expectation. Jesus said we must *love* our enemies.
10. God can love me the way I am, because he has no plan to leave me the way I am.

Questions for Further Thought

- Why do you think people loved Frank Sinatra so much when he sang, "I did it my way"?
- What should we do when we don't like the way God seems to be leading us?

Attitude of Gratitude

The lame man at the Temple gate had been there for years, begging for a few coins that gave him a meager existence. Why hadn't the man reached out to Jesus when he came by? Perhaps because others in the crowd gave him coins.

Peter came by and gave him something much more valuable.

If you who are evil know how to give good gifts to your children, you can be sure your heavenly Father will give the Holy Spirit to those who ask him.
— Luke 11:13

Ten Thoughts to Ponder

1. Being thankful becomes idolatry when we appreciate God's gifts more than the giver.
2. We have an attitude of ingratitude when we fail to recognize the value of God's gifts.
3. Every day, I have an opportunity to see more of what God has for me to see.
4. If we don't know where we are, we certainly cannot know how to get where we need to be.
5. To focus upon the details that matter, I must avoid focus upon the details that don't matter.
6. Saying we have no choice relieves us of the responsibility of making a better choice.
7. Heartfelt stories may be copied and revised, but artificial intelligence will never excel above God-given creativity.
8. The increase of knowledge is directly proportional to the recognition of our ignorance.
9. For me to know that something is a certainty merely requires believing that my perception is a certainty.
10. Independent from God, we think we know, but actually, we only know what we think.

Questions for Further Thought

- What can we expect the gift of God's presence to do for us?
- How can we show our gratitude for what we've been given?

Miracle Water

Holy water is blessed by a priest for cleansing and protection from evil. It isn't for drinking like the water at Jacob's well at Sychar. It isn't for quenching our spiritual thirst like the water Jesus offered the woman who came to draw water there.

The water of the Holy Spirit will cleanse, protect, and satisfy us better than anything else.

> *Those who drink the water I give will never become thirsty. My water is a fresh artesian spring, bubbling with everlasting life.*
> *— John 4:14*

Ten Thoughts to Ponder

1. The difference between athletes embracing or avoiding pain depends on believing the suffering is necessary to gain the possible prize.
2. Effective communication comes from the feelings behind the words, which makes the choice of words and their arrangement most crucial.
3. Knowledge is a water well. Understanding is the means to get a drink. Wisdom is quenching our thirst.
4. With God's help, I can use the oyster process to turn an irritant into a priceless pearl.
5. The future will always be unreachable, because what we have is limited to today.
6. When God lets me have my way, I learn what not to do.
7. God reverses gravity, for what goes down must go up.
8. If God causes all things to work for good, then the present must be better than the past, and the future will be better than the present, no matter what we think of "the good old days."
9. People listen with their perspectives, not the speaker's.
10. God wants to change me to what he wants, because that would make me the best I could be.

Questions for Further Thought

- Where do we get the miracle water Jesus has for us?
- What makes the miracle water permanently satisfying?

Power in Numbers

Sometimes when people go out alone, they are never heard from again. Gang members can feel safe for as long as they don't face a bigger, more powerful gang. No wonder people are afraid. To feel safe, how big an army do we need with us?

When the Lord is fighting with you, just one of your soldiers can cause ten thousand to flee.
— *Joshua 23:10*

Ten Thoughts to Ponder

1. Where two or three are gathered, synergy can be powerful, but when God is part of our group, we have synergy on steroids.
2. The blind, deaf, and ignorant are specially equipped with God's sight, hearing, and intelligence to do his will.
3. Blind faith is imagining something that isn't there, but real faith is hearing and believing God's voice, thereby knowing the truth when we can't see the evidence.
4. God's plan for my success cannot follow the path of millionaires who describe their well devised plans that will supposedly work for everybody.
5. The greatest talent I have to offer the Lord is total surrender to his way instead of mine.
6. Failure to listen is like not being there. We don't know what we're missing.
7. Except for preparation, a promise is of no use today.
8. For all things to work together for good, I need to focus on God's purpose, not mine.
9. We can be sure God knows that the avoidance of pain is a stronger motivator than the pursuit of pleasure.
10. Hearing is something I do without thinking, requiring no action, but listening is hard work that demands my full attention, followed by action.

Questions for Further Thought

- What must we do to be sure God will fight with us?
- Why does God allow Satan to be a roaring, devouring lion?

Obituary of Significance

Methuselah was an unrighteous man who died in the year of the Great Flood, with nothing worth mentioning in 969 years. People may be famous when they die, but Jesus wasn't—not until he rose from the dead. Now, we have the opportunity to reign with him.

In all domains, Jesus now stands far above every ruler, authority,
and power, his name carrying more weight than anyone in the present age
and in all times yet to come.
— Ephesians 1:21

Ten Thoughts to Ponder
1. I dare not forget my mistakes, lest I should repeat them.
2. As we walk with the Lord, the past cannot dictate our future, for he is always doing new things.
3. If Jesus is the author and finisher of our faith, then we must be his ghostwriters.
4. If I weren't so focused on what interests me, I could listen better.
5. With an intense desire to improve, we'll recognize our weaknesses and strengths, and we'll keep finding whatever works to make us better.
6. Faith is most evident between the prayer and the answer.
7. Like a GPS, the Holy Spirit can be our guide, if we choose to listen, but his gift of free will won't let him be our chauffeur, doing the driving for us.
8. The changes God wants to make in us will require a miracle that only he is capable of doing.
9. Making every word count is much more important than counting every word.
10. By caring for others more than myself, I do much more for myself than I could do if I cared more for myself.

Questions for Further Thought

- What assurance do we have that Jesus has actually made a place for us in Heaven?
- What makes our work valuable on Earth after we're gone?

Foolish Choices

A fool is one who knows better and does it anyway. Many times, I have looked back and said to myself, *I knew better than to do that*. The choice looked okay at the time, but it was a foolish choice. I fare much better by doing what I believe is *most* pleasing to the Lord.

> *All things might be okay, but I am looking for what most pleases the Lord, because that is most beneficial. I cannot allow myself to be enslaved by social pressures or selfish desires.*
> — *1 Corinthians 6:12*

Ten Thoughts to Ponder

1. Wrestling with God should contend for whatever he wants, not for what I want or even what I *think* he wants.
2. The magnitude of God is greater than the sum of the magnitude of all the stars in the universe.
3. When I can't see where I'm going, I need God's help to be comfortable with where I'm going.
4. Since my container is far too small to contain all of God's knowledge, I must be content with his help to know whatever I need to know at the time I need to know it.
5. The magnitude of God is so great that we can spend all of eternity knowing more of him.
6. If time has a beginning, we face the unanswerable question of what existed before that.
7. A good choice isn't always the best choice.
8. Without God's guidance, I might know what is good, but I don't know what is best.
9. When my choice matches God's perfect will, I have the best choice.
10. God and I can do a better job than either one of us can do, independently.

Questions for Further Thought

- What leads people to take unnecessary risks?
- Why do some Christians do what they know won't please the Lord?

Fully Capable

The most dangerous of all God's gifts is our ability to say no to him. Freewill gave Eve the power to choose what she thought would be good for her and allowed Adam to prefer his relationship with his wife above his relationship with God.

We are fully capable of evil, but we need not worry when we depend on Christ, who makes us fully capable of all that is good.

In all situations, no matter how little or how much I have, I must depend on Christ for my strength and guidance.
— *Philippians 4:13*

Ten Thoughts to Ponder
1. To see the fulfillment of God's perfect plan, I need to abandon my imperfect plans and follow him one step at a time.
2. To help the multitude, we must care about the individual who is not ourselves.
3. When people believe a mirage, they will pursue it with the vigor of a man in the desert, dying of thirst.
4. Like a natural pearl, the beauty that God wants to create in us takes time.
5. The process of God's way in our lives contains pains that turn to pleasure when his purpose is fulfilled.
6. Miracles are proven when God's intervention is undeniable.
7. A bargain is a waste of money if it gives me something I will never use.
8. The improvements God helps me make today will benefit me for the rest of my life and beyond.
9. When everything working together for good isn't good enough, we have nowhere else to turn but to the Lord.
10. Without encouragement, we will most likely fail.

Questions for Further Thought

- What obstacles do we face in becoming fully dependent upon God for our strength and guidance?
- What did you learn from the bad choices you have made?

Unconditional Surrender

After a devastating battle with a foreign nation, no longer wanting to resist the invader, the defeated king sought favorable conditions for surrender. By serving the foreign king, the people were given life and peace. When we reject Satan's temptation for independence and unconditionally surrender to the Lord, we can enjoy his peace forever.

Completely surrender your will to whatever God wants. What you ought to say is this: "Whatever the Lord wants—that's what I live to do each day." Sin is failure to do the good you know you should do.
— James 4:7, 15, 17

Ten Thoughts to Ponder
1. To fulfill God's plan for my life, my best won't be good enough without his help.
2. I must trust the Lord's guidance, because the greatest danger comes from the threats we cannot see.
3. I respect people's opinions, even when they are wrong, for they have a God-given right to them.
4. After I give out, give in, and give up, God has what he needs in me for a miracle.
5. "I know I can't" is an important admission for making all things possible with God.
6. Since I don't understand myself well, my confidence comes from knowing that God does, and he will direct my steps.
7. Who we are is much more important than how we look.
8. With what God can do in our lives, we would rightly have a name better than the one we were given at birth.
9. If we faithfully see the process to the end, the Holy Spirit will restore us to God's image that we have lost.
10. The most magnificent self-directed plan cannot be as good as the worst of all God-directed plans.

Questions for Further Thought

- Why might people want to negotiate their conditions of surrender to the Lord?
- What treasures would you never want to give up?

Worthless Weeds

In the six days of creation, God saw that all he had made was good, meaning "perfectly suited for his purpose." In Jesus' story about the wheat, the master wouldn't allow the weeds to be pulled, because he didn't want one valuable plant to be lost. In our serving the Lord and not just ourselves, we prove that we're not worthless weeds.

Just as the weeds are bundled and burned, so will it be with people at the end of this age.
— *Matthew 13:40*

Ten Thoughts to Ponder
1. To hear more from God, spend more time talking to him and asking questions.
2. The best prayer people can offer others is asking God to be their GPS.
3. The need for "prayer without ceasing" is to live under God's constant guidance.
4. I do well to follow God's suggestions as well as his commands.
5. If we follow God's suggestions, we'll have no trouble keeping his commandments.
6. When the wrong doesn't distract us, we are free to focus on everything right.
7. If I can imagine God's greatness, my mind has severely limited who he is.
8. I want to be thankful for every contributing part of God's plan for me, no matter how painful his design might be.
9. Contrary to my limited perspective, with God I can move forward in all directions at the same time—like the explosion of the universe.
10. The nature of being God's disciple is to give up everything we have so we can have everything he has.

Questions for Further Thought

- Why do weeds thrive so well?
- What conditions do we need to grow in Christ?

Wash Up

When called to dinner, I wasn't allowed at the table until I had washed my hands with soap and water. Sometimes, I had to wash my face as well. According to my mother, "Cleanliness was next to godliness." What was the problem? I'd had a bath the night before.

When coming in from a dirty world, clean people need to wash up.

Since we are promised this relationship with God, let's cleanse ourselves from all filth, both physical and spiritual, respecting who he is and wanting to be like him.
— 2 Corinthians 7:1

Ten Thoughts to Ponder

1. As we walk with the Lord, what others see as problems are our opportunities.
2. A working writer doesn't complain about God's assignments.
3. A goal without conscious pursuit is meaningless fantasy.
4. Like electricity, we don't have to understand God to flip the switch and have the light come on.
5. I don't know. I think I know but don't. I think I don't know but do. Those are three good reasons why I need God's guidance, because without him, I don't know enough.
6. When I move closer to the Lord, I can hear him better.
7. Because we live in a filthy world, we should frequently wash up and feast upon God's Word.
8. A move toward God is a step in the right direction, but to walk close to him, we must avoid distractions and stay focused on wherever he wants us to go.
9. To deliver God's message effectively, we must be listening.
10. Inspiration has little value without perspiration.

Questions for Further Thought

- How much scrubbing do we really need before we are completely clean?
- Why are some people concerned about their appearance but not who they are on the inside?

Cheap Knockoff

Sceva had seven sons who studied the apostle Paul's methods in delivering people from demons. They knew exactly what to say. But there was a problem. Without the Holy Spirit behind their words, they had no power over the forces of evil.

A religious form might seem real to those who blindly follow a liturgy, but it will never fool the Lord.

> *They have a religious form with only a façade of righteousness, not the Holy Spirit acting with power in their lives. Do not fellowship with these people.*
> — *2 Timothy 3:5*

Ten Thoughts to Ponder
1. Watching the clock is a needless waste of time.
2. Wild, unruly hair may make you look like Einstein, but it won't make you any smarter.
3. If we *think* we know, we should still wonder if we *really do*.
4. When not having what I want is a necessity, I need to be satisfied with the dissatisfaction.
5. No matter how hard I try to succeed, I'm sure to fail without God's help. But in working to fulfill his purpose in my life, the only way I can fail is to quit.
6. When I do nothing, the results are guaranteed.
7. Today is the most important day of my life, because I can do nothing about the past, and I can do nothing about the future until it arrives.
8. Having done all we know to do, we desperately need God's help to know what more to do.
9. Were it not for the tests, I would have no testimony.
10. We think we know what we need, but God knows better.

Questions for Further Thought
- How do we know that our relationship with the Lord is real, and we have a place reserved for us in Heaven?
- Why are some people satisfied with a knockoff instead of owning the real thing?

Meeting in Heaven

Many songs remind me of the day when I will see Jesus. The older I get, the more I long to see friends and family who are in Heaven, awaiting my arrival. I'd like to see Peter, John, and the apostle Paul. I want to hear stories from Abraham, Moses, and Elijah. Of all the biblical characters, who do you most want to see besides Jesus?

I want to see the widow who Jesus saw in the Temple so I can learn what was so valuable that she gave everything she had.

> *Jesus said, "There are many places where you can stay in my Father's house. After I have prepared for your arrival, I will come back for you so we can be there together."*
> — *John 14:1, 3*

Ten Thoughts to Ponder

1. We would say more, or less, if we knew what the Lord wanted us to say, which is why we should pray without ceasing.
2. Possessing God's blessings is nothing to boast about, for their value comes from giving, not getting.
3. We don't have to *define* God before we can *experience* and *know* him.
4. A strong-willed person can resist scratching an itch.
5. Complacency will yield to a distraction without even knowing it has.
6. Surprise is a magician pulling a dog out of a rabbit's hat.
7. Without direction, subconscious thinking becomes an accident.
8. Delight comes from not having to wait any longer.
9. If we understand that God is supplying our needs, we can delight in him because we don't have to wait any longer.
10. Intentional distractions are willful detours from what we know we should be doing.

Questions for Further Thought

- What might your checkbook and credit card statements say about what you value most?
- What will you say to the first person you meet in Heaven?

Defying Gravity

In my dreams, I can defy gravity, floating above buildings like a hot-air balloon, able to go where I please and do whatever I imagine. When I'm awake, I depend upon the Lord to lift me up and take me to wherever he wants me to go.

Your Word is a lamp to keep my feet from stumbling, a light that shines before me to show the way you want me to go.
— Psalm 119:105

Ten Thoughts to Ponder

1. Magic is an outcome where conditions should have produced a different result. Miracles are whenever God intervenes.
2. The difference between results and consequences is whether we care about what our actions produce.
3. When I do what God wants, I don't have to worry about the results, but when I don't do what God wants, I have reason to be concerned about the consequences.
4. If I love God and I'm working to fulfill his purpose, the results will be good, even when I think the conditions are bad.
5. The only way to guarantee results is to quit.
6. Sometimes I try to sense what my true sense is, but I don't have enough sense. So I need God's sense, or I'm flat broke.
7. If I could know the way things really are, I might know what I really need. Since I don't know, I must trust the Lord for what he knows I need.
8. What I call a lack of motivation is actually a motivation *not to do* what I would otherwise be motivated to do.
9. Conclusive evidence only appears to be conclusive when we lack information that would change our conclusions.
10. A goal has value only if what we are doing right now is focused in the right direction.

Questions for Further Thought

- What darkens people's paths so they don't know what to do?
- When we don't know where to go or what to do, how can we turn on the light and see better?

Play for Pay

In grade school, my favorite class was recess. At home, I had chores that had to be done before I could go out to play. Later, I would never have taken a job if it hadn't been for the pay that let me have fun. Now, I'm so thankful to have learned how much fun work can be. When I'm pleasing the Lord, work is like fishing for a living.

> *"Come, follow me," Jesus said, "and I will make you fishers of men."*
> — *Matthew 4:19*

Ten Thoughts to Ponder

1. If I think I know all that God wants to do, I am most certainly wrong. The only question is to what extent.
2. We should have much greater delight in walking with the Lord than in having him walk with us.
3. Having to change is the harsh reality of self-improvement, which can be difficult to accept when we love our old selves.
4. An important part of learning is unlearning what we thought was right, but it wasn't.
5. Admitting that we don't know is a childhood strength that adults need for growth.
6. Because anything we want to know can be quickly looked up on the Internet, we live in an age where learning and remembering doesn't matter much.
7. By creating false memories, people change the past that they want to forget.
8. Other people's successes cannot be a model for my success, because God's plan for me is different.
9. I need to remove the pieces in my puzzle that don't fit. I just *think* they do. If only I could identify which ones they are.
10. I prefer what God really wants for me rather than to have what I *imagine* that he wants.

Questions for Further Thought

- Why do most employees dislike the work they do?
- What can you do to have more fun while you work?

Open Doors

What's the difference between temptations, trials, and triumphs? All are available through open doors that we might or might not want to enter, if only we could know what lies on the other side.

This is why I often pray, "Lord, please don't open a door that you don't want me to walk through, because you know how dumb I am."

You will hear a voice behind you, saying, "This is the way to go. Walk in that direction," and you will turn to the right or left as you are led.
— *Isaiah 30:21*

Ten Thoughts to Ponder
1. An eagerness to learn opens many doors for discovery.
2. People's perception of reality turns upside down when they see cause as the effect and the effect as the cause.
3. Like Peter walking on water, our stability depends on our focus upon the Lord's command to "come."
4. A huge toolbox has no value unless the Lord helps me know which tool is needed and helps me use it.
5. The better we know God, the more we can trust him.
6. Being used of God for his good purpose changes our value from worthless to priceless.
7. If we think we must understand God before we can trust him, we will never be able to trust him.
8. What God doesn't do is as significant as what he does.
9. If God cares enough to see every sparrow that falls, we should know he cares about us and knows everything we think, say, and do—for we are worth much more than two sparrows.
10. As a computer has dozens of unseen tasks going on in the background, we can't see what God is working to cause all things to work together for good.

Questions for Further Thought
- How much do our motives matter in deciding whether an open door is an opportunity and not a danger?
- What did you learn after a good choice turned out to be bad?

Treasure or Trash

Where is my old stamp collection that taught me more about geography than any class at school? What happened to my box of baseball cards, old coins, and Indian relics?

I have lost, given away, or thrown away many things I would like to have today. I'm still learning the difference between treasure and trash.

Store your treasure in Heaven, where it is safe from moths and rust and thieves. Wherever your treasure is, there your heart will be also.
— Matthew 6:20–21

Ten Thoughts to Ponder
1. By giving up my treasures, I live God's treasures instead.
2. Sidetracks and detours are wonderful only when they come as a result of God's guidance, not my self-serving desires.
3. I can easily be thankful for past miracles in my life, but I need the Lord's strength to face the challenges and trials that let me experience more miracles ahead.
4. Seeking the Lord is difficult, because we need the Lord's help to do it.
5. I'm deceiving myself if I have a goal and don't take another step in that direction each day.
6. With God's vision, I can know when a step back is necessary to move forward.
7. I'm thankful that God understands me better than what my words can express.
8. Thoughts unexpressed are either unknown treasures or trash.
9. Like Peter who needed Jesus' hand to walk on water, we need God's help to rise above our problems and not drown.
10. Even the least-significant wish that God might have concerning me belongs on my list of great prayer needs.

Questions for Further Thought

- Why might air and water be more valuable than diamonds and gold?
- When might your great loss have turned out to be great gain?

Reading the Signs

On a bitterly cold day, I left Daddy to his exploring the hillside while I returned to the car to get warm. Oh, no! The gas gauge needle was on empty. I bawled. We were so many miles from civilization. I was sure we would either freeze to death or die of starvation.

I didn't know the gas tank would read half full if the ignition switch was turned on. I wasn't even in kindergarten yet, but I was old enough to learn that I needed help to correctly read the signs and know the truth.

> *You can look at the sky and predict the weather, but you cannot interpret the signs of the times.*
> — *Matthew 16:3*

Ten Thoughts to Ponder
1. To discover the right answer, one must ask lots of questions.
2. The problem with obvious conclusions is the right conclusion not being as obvious as we think it is.
3. Since just one complaint can destroy a thousand compliments, we certainly need God's help for one to chase a thousand and two to cause ten thousand to flee.
4. We need *faith* to accept what God wants to work in us.
5. The faith that moves mountains is much more important in areas beyond the most obvious, physical realm.
6. Great ideas are worthless if they're never put to use.
7. If I don't do the work God had for me to do yesterday, I'm running behind with the work I need to do today.
8. Since God has everything we need, looking elsewhere is a great resource for finding what can never satisfy.
9. The truth has no value unless people are willing to believe it.
10. A lack of answers is why I pray a lot.

Questions for Further Thought
- When was the last time you misread a sign and went some distance before you realized you had taken a wrong turn?
- Why don't other people sometimes fail to see the truth that is so obvious to you?

Available Tools

At 2:00 a.m., far away from the nearest town, our church bus was taking snow skiers to the Rockies. Bam! A blowout. Now, a problem. The tire tool refused to loosen the lug nuts. We were stuck. Then I noticed the speed-limit sign bent over slightly, at just the right angle for three men to pull down on the pipe slipped over the tire tool.

To accomplish what God wants, tools are always available.

> God said to Moses, "Take your staff in your hand and use it."
> — Exodus 4:17

Ten Thoughts to Ponder

1. What appears to be an extremely valuable tool is actually worthless if it is never used.
2. Artificial intelligence will never match God's creative might that can work through us.
3. A word from the Lord is better than a counselor's advice.
4. If we lack faith, then we either haven't heard God's voice, or we haven't believed him. If we don't lack faith but think we do, then our faith is not yet brought us to obedience.
5. I must always make time to do whatever I feel like the Lord would have me do.
6. I must have confidence that the Lord is in control of whatever needs to happen, so I can have confidence in doing whatever he has for me to do.
7. When God's thoughts are not my thoughts, my desires are led astray.
8. The only thing I seem to know without any question is my ability to ask questions.
9. My perception of reality falls far short of what God knows, which leaves me dependent upon him to direct my steps.
10. One amazing ability we have in our growth with God is an ability to move forward in all directions at the same time.

Questions for Further Thought

- When have you used a tool for an unintended purpose?
- How do we make ourselves available for God's use?

Blame Game

At work, I never understood how my being one day late getting an production order written could be why Manufacturing was four weeks late. Evidently, an *illogical* excuse was better than taking all the blame.

I still had to admit my small contribution to the delay.

> *"The woman you made to be my companion gave me the fruit,"*
> *Adam said, "and I ate it."*
> *The woman said, "The snake deceived me. That's why I ate it.*
> *— Genesis 3:12*

Ten Thoughts to Ponder
1. If we could see people the way God sees people, we would know how much he cares.
2. Uncontrolled anger causes murder by whatever means is available, so holding the weapon responsible is foolishness.
3. What we love is not necessarily what we say it is. It's actually revealed by what we do—whatever we surrender ourselves to.
4. Because God wants the very best for me, he can't always do what I pray for him to do.
5. Before we can know how to *give* love, we must know how to *receive* it.
6. To have faith and yield to God's will, I must hear his voice.
7. If I feel like I'm in control, I've not yet fully surrendered control of my life to the Lord.
8. Our greatest satisfaction comes from knowing we have done exactly what the Lord wanted.
9. Without the Lord's help, my words cannot be as good as they need to be to fulfill his purpose.
10. Starting is easy, but without patience and persistence, finishing is impossible.

Questions for Further Thought
- Why do people so often blame others for their bad choices?
- What do we have to gain by admitting our mistakes and taking responsibility for our actions?

Real Hope

Robert Schuller wrote many bestselling books about *Possibility Thinking*. Something about that message must have been real, or so many people wouldn't have kept coming back to hear more.

For those who don't know the Lord, possibility thinking can't be any better than false hope. Among all the things that might seem good, the suffering ahead is a *reality*, not just a *possibility*. For those of us who belong to Christ, we can ignore the present darkness because our future is brighter than anything we can imagine.

May your God, who has given you eager anticipation for the future, give you peace and joy right now as you trust in him. Then the Holy Spirit will give you even more confidence in where you are headed.
— Romans 15:13

Ten Thoughts to Ponder

1. If I choose always to walk with the Lord, continuous improvement is inevitable.
2. Hope is ... Having Our Patience Energized.
3. Eyeglasses won't help me when my eyes are closed.
4. Like the ladder can have only one top rung, of all the good things we could do, only one thing is most pleasing to the Lord.
5. To walk in the Spirit, we must pray without ceasing.
6. I am thankful that God will answer the important questions that I didn't know to ask.
7. If we aren't yet where we need to be, and we don't know how to get there, we need answers that only God can provide.
8. Insanity is thinking my way could be better than God's way.
9. To remain discouraged, I must ignore God's encouraging words.
10. In seeking the truth, I must first admit that I don't know.

Questions for Further Thought

- What might lead Christians to believe their situation is hopeless?
- How can we strengthen our hope in Christ?

Fairest of All

To the question, "Who's the fairest of them all," the magic mirror's answer should have been: *The Photoshopped picture from the best of a hundred shots taken in the ideal pose and perfect light.* That image is nowhere close to who we will be when the Holy Spirit finishes his work.

> *Like someone looking into a mirror, we see the beauty of who we will become, more and more like the Lord, being changed from glory to even greater glory by the work of his Spirit.*
> — *2 Corinthians 3:18*

Ten Thoughts to Ponder
1. Profound thoughts often state the obvious that we hadn't stopped to notice.
2. A strong desire might do the impossible, but it cannot do what it does not want to do.
3. To be God's friend, we must want what he wants.
4. Since reality doesn't depend upon my reasoning, it might not make sense to me unless God helps me understand.
5. Adjustments are needed now, or they will be part of either the unchangeable past or the future that may never arrive.
6. Genius is learning from our experiences and receiving help from others, especially the Lord. Then I can be the "me" with life-changing experiences that people want to read about.
7. When Solomon said, "There's nothing new under the sun," he couldn't see all the things that God hadn't yet done.
8. As the Lord makes me a "new creature," I won't be like anybody else. But I will be in *his* "likeness."
9. If I am to believe I cannot fail, that trust must rely upon the Lord, not upon my strength.
10. What we *think* we know can be a significant obstacle in acquiring more of what we *need* to know.

Questions for Further Thought

- What is the difference between *looking* great and *being* great?
- How can we "let our light shine" so people look at us and recognize the glory of our Creator?

Seasoned Veteran

In facing Goliath, David is often pictured as a child, but actually he was tall enough for Saul to offer his armor and had to be much older than when David played the harp and was an armor bearer. After Goliath fell, Saul had to ask who David was.

To Goliath, David looked like a child, but he was actually a seasoned veteran after killing the lion and the bear.

As mature adults can chew tough meat, those who have been through a lot have their spiritual senses exercised to distinguish between right and wrong choices.
— Hebrews 5:14

Ten Thoughts to Ponder

1. Without God, I don't know where I am, where to go, or how to get there.
2. Imagination can show what looks good but might be fatal.
3. The desire to do what's right needs to be stronger than the desire to avoid pain or pursue pleasure.
4. Dilemmas are most easily solved by incorrect assumptions, without the hard work to be sure of the truth.
5. Close your eyes or look the other way—that's the best way to wind up in the ditch.
6. God's truth sets us free because we are no longer tugged in opposite directions, unable to decide which way is right.
7. When God gave us a choice, he made us responsible for decisions he will not control, yet he still has the power to make everything work for good.
8. In choosing what pleases the Lord, our desire to do right must be stronger than avoiding pain or pursuing pleasure.
9. To accomplish something important, we must abandon the unimportant.
10. To have a friend, you must be a friend to many.

Questions for Further Thought

- What battles have given you spiritual strength?
- For what reasons should we be thankful for tough times?

Bumpy Ride

Wanting to spend time with my son, I planned a weekend fishing trip, which was disaster from the start. He didn't want to go, and he did nothing but complain as we drove to the lake. On the walk out to the end of the pier, he talked like this had to be the worst day of his life. Reluctantly, he took the pole and dropped the baited hook into the water. Moments later, he felt a tug on the line, reeled in the fish, and said, "Dad, this is fun."

If we can trust where the Lord is leading us, we can enjoy the ride and have lots of fun when we get there.

> *Jesus said, "I am the light of the world. Those who follow me will never walk in darkness, because they have the light of life."*
> *— John 8:12*

Ten Thoughts to Ponder

1. Asking for help is good, because it recognizes a need. *Getting* help is better—when it *meets* that need.
2. My memory works great as long as I make a note—and remember to check my notes.
3. With questions, we relieve the pain of our ignorance.
4. The most dangerous influences are those we don't recognize.
5. If I can't do the work, and I must rely upon the Lord. He will turn my "I can't" into "I can."
6. By growing our good addictions, our bad addictions can lose their grip on our lives.
7. Knowing the good doesn't help unless it is followed by doing the good.
8. Bad habits can only be eliminated by replacing them with better alternatives.
9. In caring for others, I need to be more excited and concerned for them than I am for myself.
10. Idolatry is *imagining* God instead of *knowing* God.

Questions for Further Thought

- Why might people be reluctant to walk with God?
- In being with the Lord, what is *most* enjoyable?

Point of No Return

I hoped the driver could handle deep snow, because we already had several inches covering the road. The farther we went, the deeper the drifts, until the windblown edge was our only way to know where the pavement ended and the ditch began.

"Shall we turn back?" the driver said.

Silly question. Going back wouldn't get us to the ski slopes, where we wanted to go.

> *"After a man puts his hand to the plow," Jesus said, "he is not fit for the Kingdom of God if he keeps looking back."*
> — *Luke 9:62*

Ten Thoughts to Ponder

1. In complete surrender to the Lord, failure is never final. It's a steppingstone for guaranteed success.
2. The exciting thing about picking up a tool comes from knowing what can be accomplished.
3. Foolishness is saying I need something from the Lord when I already have it but don't use it.
4. We need a special talent from the Lord to convince people of what they *don't* believe.
5. If whatever we are doing isn't working, it's time to look to the Lord for a better sense of direction—and be patient.
6. I need to forget everything that needs to be forgotten so I can remember everything that needs to be remembered.
7. Giving up is the best way to be a victim rather than a victor.
8. Becoming the person God wants us to be cannot happen without both our agreement and his power.
9. If all things are to work together for good, then both God and I must be relentless in our pursuit of all that is good.
10. When the storm surrounds us, turning back is not an option.

Questions for Further Thought

- As we move forward, why might looking back be a problem?
- What should we do with obstacles that either hinder us or prevent us from moving forward?

Change of Scenery

Every morning, I walked to the park and counted each time I circled the pond until my mileage goal was met. After a year, I'd seen it all—or so I thought. One day, I decided to circle the pond in the opposite direction and was amazed at how much I'd never noticed before.

We need God's perspective to see things as they really are.

Elisha prayed, saying, "Lord, open his eyes so he can see." The Lord opened the young man's eyes, and he saw the mountain filled with horses and chariots of fire all around them.
— 2 Kings 6:17

Ten Thoughts to Ponder

1. Minor improvements build toward major achievements.
2. With closed eyes, I see my thoughts more clearly.
3. Love can appreciate others without saying they won't be loved if they are different from who we are.
4. I'm thankful for my discomfort, because otherwise I might not make the changes God wants.
5. If I spend very little time on what's not worthwhile, I have a lot of time to do worthwhile things.
6. With high expectations, I set myself up for feelings of rejection and discouragement after the Lord leads me in an unexpected direction.
7. When God made us with a deep desire to be loved and appreciated, he also created a need that only he could completely satisfy.
8. Obedience is simple. Just do it. The complicated part is not wanting to do it.
9. Disappointment comes from trying to please others, not God.
10. God knows how we feel, because he has experienced rejection more than anybody on Earth.

Questions for Further Thought

- What is the difference between routines, ruts, and grooves?
- How can we appreciate what the Lord has for us when we have never seen it?

Breaking Burnout

After teaching Sunday school for ten years, Charlie said he was just worn out and couldn't teach anymore. Why? Burnout. Obviously, he was overloaded with responsibilities and needed to cut back.

Actually, his burnout wasn't from being overworked. He allowed the fire of the Spirit to be snuffed out. The glorious vision was lost.

Never tire of doing good, for a harvest of blessing is certain if you never give up on God.
— *Galatians 6:9*

Ten Thoughts to Ponder
1. God didn't make robots, and he didn't give us artificial intelligence.
2. Persistence in following God is our choice, not something that God is willing to force upon us.
3. In refusing to give up, I must follow God's better plan because my plan is clearly not working.
4. All that God has done for us gives us the perfect reason to hope for more.
5. Some people claim righteousness they don't have, making it impossible to acquire the righteousness they are claiming.
6. The best way to profit from doing nothing is to get some sleep and be energized for the next thing that must be done.
7. The greatness of God may be beyond explanation, but he is not beyond experience that goes on forever.
8. The explosion of God's voice deserves an eruption of wild, colorful, spectacular words.
9. Eliminating a weakness is a doubled benefit because a strength is no longer drained to cover the weakness.
10. Foolishness is wanting to run when God wants to walk with us—or wanting to run when he wants to walk.

Questions for Further Thought

- How can we stir up God's gift of his presence so his vision will burn brighter in us than ever before?
- How can doing less allow more of what's most important?

Making the Grade

Since I loved math and science, I learned everything I could and didn't worry about the tests. English and history were boring, so I only cared about making a good grade. I reviewed the material ahead of time, aced the tests, and left the classes remembering nothing.

If I want to pass whatever tests God has for me, I need to listen and learn very well.

Study diligently so you will be recognized by God and others as one who correctly interprets Scripture, one who need not be ashamed.
— *2 Timothy 2:15*

Ten Thoughts to Ponder

1. Sometimes it takes more energy to be silent than to speak up.
2. If we are filled with God's presence, we are safe in expressing whatever comes to mind.
3. Not wanting to do something I want to do can be a confusing, energy-killing dilemma.
4. The right motivation is important, or our energy will be focused in the wrong direction.
5. Nothing is permanent unless it goes on forever, and that's an immeasurably long time.
6. Doing things right the first time is much less costly than having to make adjustments.
7. If we want tomorrow to be different from what it would otherwise be, something needs to change today.
8. The future is a mystery filled with questions where I must depend on God for the answers.
9. I am looking for the one special answer that solves the great problem I don't even know I have.
10. We don't have to be content with good, because we can enjoy God's best when we have totally surrendered to his will.

Questions for Further Thought

- How important is reading the Bible?
- If we fail one of God's tests, what is the likelihood that we will have to take the test again?

Unseen Danger

On the way to making the next delivery, I headed toward the intersection. Whap! My feet hit the brakes. Why? The traffic light was green. Then I saw the pickup speeding across the intersection, right where I should have been.

Without God's vision, the dangers we don't see can kill us.

The angel of the Lord stands guard around those who revere God, and he delivers them.
— Psalm 34:7

Ten Thoughts to Ponder

1. We will achieve more if we can worry less about results and focus more on effort in doing whatever God wants.
2. God is the greatest source of creativity in the universe.
3. Two things that seem not connected at all can actually be inseparably linked, each one depending upon the other.
4. Finding things is amazingly easy when you look in the right place—and impossible, otherwise.
5. Anticipation of greater things can distract me from what I need to do now to make the greater things possible.
6. When I don't know what question to ask, I am even more dependent upon God for answers.
7. The problem with guessing is the risk of being wrong when I think I am right.
8. What I accomplish is dependent upon my actions, not by my ability.
9. The future is for God to know now and for me to find out when I get there.
10. Progress must recognize changes and adjust to what is different from what it was before.

Questions for Further Thought

- How can we keep from worrying about all the dangers we can't see?
- If Satan roams the world, seeking whom he can devour, what keeps us from being his next victim?

Fear of Dying

You may have heard the inspiring historical reports of bullet holes through George Washington's uniform, which can't be explained since no bullet ever wounded him. I don't know if those stories are true, but I'm sure they could be. I've lost count of the number of times I either *could* or *should* have died.

Most people fear dying—and for good reason if they don't know the Lord. But the better question is to ask the Lord, "Why am I still here on Earth?"

> *We are God's creative masterpiece, brought to life in Jesus Christ so we can do the great work he designed for us in the beginning.*
> — *Ephesians 2:10*

Ten Thoughts to Ponder
1. Dreams are the most fantastic when they become reality.
2. No desire of ours is capable of reproducing what only God can do.
3. An inch away from what the Lord wants might as well be as distant as a mile if I don't have his help to get there.
4. It doesn't rain every day—except when it rains every day.
5. Many people want to identify as someone they are not, yet that would be a good thing if they wanted to identify as the new creature that God wants them to be.
6. With God's help, we can do much more than what we can do.
7. Relaxed in the Lord, I am never wound up and don't have to take time to unwind.
8. I need to be more captivated by whatever the Lord wants me to be captivated by.
9. The blame belongs to me, and all the credit belongs to the Lord.
10. I need more of God's desire and less of mine.

Questions for Further Thought

- When might the Lord have kept you from dying, and you didn't even know he was present to do that miracle?
- What parts of God's purpose are yet to be completed?

Puzzle Mania

Working picture puzzles is something like fishing. *Looking* is good, but *finding* is a greater thrill. For a long time at my house, putting a puzzle together has been a family tradition. At Christmas, before I remove the wrapping paper, the sound, feel, and shape of the gift tell me I'm about to be delighted with another puzzle.

Sometimes, I'm so sure a piece should fit, I'm tempted to look for a hammer. Like truth, when I've not found it, I must keep looking.

> *People with discerning hearts seek the truth, but fools are satisfied with whatever sounds good.*
> — *Proverbs 15:14*

Ten Thoughts to Ponder

1. Having tried and failed, I obviously need God's help in trying again—or knowing I shouldn't try.
2. In wanting to know and saying so, I admit my ignorance and my need to know.
3. Having done all I know to do, there is nothing else to do but persist in waiting and seek to discover what I should do.
4. What we put in our stomachs may affect our dreams at night, but not as much as what we've seen and heard during the day.
5. When I don't take credit for my success, I get to enjoy more of the Lord as my reason for success.
6. Despite evidence to the contrary, the right desire will produce the right results when God is the force behind the desire.
7. Without change, progress is an absolute impossibility.
8. Since we so easily miss the obvious, recognizing what we should already know can seem profound.
9. Repeating only what I've done before is insufficient proof that I am doing better.
10. Doing things together is a wonderful way to put things together.

Questions for Further Thought

- What answer did you discover that was really exciting?
- Why might we find pleasure in solving puzzles?

Setting a Deadline

A *deadline* is the "line" I decide I can't cross, or I would be dead. Stated another way, it's the time I must act, or I'm already too late. For my ten-page American History term paper, my deadline to start was Sunday evening after church. I was up until 3:00 a.m. so the thrown-together manuscript was ready for my first-period class.

Since any future moment might be too late, my deadline for greater surrender to the Lord is always now.

> *Everyone who not only hears my words but also puts them into practice is like a wise man who dug deep and laid the foundation of his house on solid rock.*
> — *Matthew 7:24*

Ten Thoughts to Ponder
1. Not knowing and not believing I can learn is a frustrating effort-killer that will destroy my productivity.
2. A perfectionist sees a 100 grade as success and 99 as failure. But 70 percent is success when 69 is seen as failure.
3. God wants our best, because our best is what's best for us.
4. The best way to feel good is to be good to others.
5. If we want to know what God wants, we should be asking.
6. Bad things become good when God works them together to fulfill his purpose.
7. Our most challenging wrestling matches are those we have with ourselves.
8. The difficulty with a bad choice is its appearance of being good.
9. If I feel I don't know, that's my reality, even though it might not be true.
10. The most backward desire is trying to make God want whatever we want.

Questions for Further Thought

- Why do people procrastinate and wind up being late?
- What steps are necessary to always meet deadlines and avoid embarrassment?

Big Payoff

One dollar doesn't sound like a big investment. Could I afford *three*? While attending a seminar in Las Vegas, I was walking around the hotel. I couldn't believe the size of the *Big Bertha* slot machine. It only took one-dollar coins, so I cashed a five-dollar bill, dropped in a coin, and pulled the handle. When the spinning wheels stopped, the numbers lined up: 7-7-7. Where was the million-dollar payoff? Then I read the label. For any payoff, I needed three dollars, not one.

For my big payoff with the Lord, I need to be all-in.

> *Jesus said, "If you are not ready to give up everything you have, you cannot be my disciple."*
> — *Luke 14:33*

Ten Thoughts to Ponder
1. Lazy minds *love* artificial intelligence, and ignorant minds have reason to *fear* it.
2. Regression is growth in the wrong direction.
3. If I am sure that God knows my needs better than I do, then his provision is better than I think.
4. When I need help, the huge question is, what should I do?
5. When I am in the most desperate need, what I most need is to rely upon the Lord.
6. Truth can only be explained. It is neither *established* nor *dependent* upon we *think* Scripture means.
7. The answer I most need is how to approach the Lord to receive an answer.
8. No matter how much we try to make it so, *artificial* will never be the *real* thing.
9. God can attain a level of perfection in me that is far above anything I can do on my own.
10. Right answers are easily missed when I'm not asking the right questions.

Questions for Further Thought

- What kind of gamble is giving up everything for the Lord?
- Why might people want to negotiate with God?

Winning Chance

My best friend and I were well-matched, both physically and academically. Walking home, we found a can on the roadside and took turns kicking it, seeing who could give it just the right spin to make it stand on end. Since neither of us won or lost all the time, we kept playing the game.

One day while seeing who could leap the farthest, I soared two feet farther than either of us had gone before. Both of us knew we'd never beat that distance. We never played that game again.

Don't be too quick to give up, but allow the situation to bring maturity, strength, and contentment.
— *James 1:4*

Ten Thoughts to Ponder
1. Not having the answer is never a good excuse to quit looking.
2. Assurance that what I believe is true must come from the Lord, because I have no means to be confident in my own, independent perspective.
3. Without listening, there is no learning.
4. If there is no learning, my mistakes are sure to be repeated.
5. If I could know all that God has done for me, I'd be too busy praising him to ever complain.
6. Since God can never lie, I can depend on his guidance—unless I lie to myself.
7. When people ask a question, I can answer immediately—because I don't mind being wrong.
8. If I have what God knows I need for the present moment, I have no need to regret the past or worry about the future.
9. I want to know God's truth, because *my* truth isn't good enough.
10. My only competitive interest is to become the person God wants me to be. That would be the greatest victory of all.

Questions for Further Thought
- Why do people compete if they know they can't win?
- When we have lost, how might the Lord have won?

Bargain Hunter

Inflation has raised many costs but none as much as the sky-high claims of value. Occasionally, we'll still see a 50 percent value gained by buying one and getting a second one free.

The latest trend in great marketing is to offer something that will make you rich—a training program worth $9,000 that only costs $197 if you buy now. Who could refuse that? What a deal.

Actually, no deal is a bargain if we're not going to use what we've paid for.

Be generous in giving of what you have received, as good servants who demonstrate the abundance of God's grace.
— *1 Peter 4:10*

Ten Thoughts to Ponder

1. My vision for yesterday no longer matters. Now I need to anticipate what God might have for me today.
2. Patience is the testing of our faith.
3. Knowing my need leaves me dependent upon the Lord isn't when he's the only one who has the answer.
4. I was in trouble when I didn't know the truth. I'm still in trouble if I don't know why it's true.
5. Until I've done for the Lord all I can with all I have, I can't justify complaining to him about not having enough.
6. I want what God *knows* I need, not what I *think* I need.
7. Our disabilities can either be an incentive to do more or an excuse to do less.
8. A great strength can also be a challenging weakness.
9. Too much of a good thing can be a bad thing.
10. My ability to do everything God wants me to do forces me to deny the *disability* that says I don't have the ability.

Questions for Further Thought

- Why do people fill storage facilities with goods they've not used in ten years and probably won't use in ten more?
- What obstacles keep you from making better use of your talents in fulfilling God's purpose for your life?

Seeing Ghosts

Daddy turned off the light and told me to go to sleep.

The dim light from the hallway cast scary shadows. I'd never been attacked by a ghost, but I knew they were there. Monsters were hiding under the bed or lurking behind the curtains. I screamed.

Daddy took me by the hand and led me through the darkness. Checked the curtains. Looked under the bed. I knew I was safe because Daddy was there.

> *As I walk through the most trying times of my life, a dark valley of the shadow of death, I still don't have to fear, because you're at my side.*
> — *Psalm 23:4*

Ten Thoughts to Ponder

1. Unlike Jesus, who only listened to his Father, the apostle Paul had to un-learn much of what he had been taught.
2. I must understand a little, or I don't know what question to ask so I could understand more.
3. If I didn't want to know, that I wouldn't have to wonder why and ask so many questions.
4. Fear is wonderful if we fear the right things—and *paralyzing* if we don't.
5. Faith is more than believing. It's the *result* of believing, the *knowing* that is seen in our actions.
6. I'm not smart enough to know how ignorant I am, but thankfully, God is.
7. The *very bestest* is immeasurably better than *just gooder.*
8. To have focus, I must at least be looking toward the target. Only then can I aim at the bull's-eye.
9. When things are going well, my greatest need is to remember how desperately I need the Lord's help.
10. God's control of my life is still incomplete at 99.9 percent.

Questions for Further Thought

- Why do we imagine dangers that aren't there while not seeing dangers that are?
- How can people avoid their fear of death?

Planting Seeds

I was four years old when Daddy told me to go down the furrow, drop beans the width of my hand apart, and cover them up. Then the miracle would happen. A plant would come up with *lots* of beans.

Three days later, I had my doubts, so I went to our garden to dig down to see. Sure enough, that bean had sprouted. It was growing!

He who plants a few seeds will have a small harvest. But he who plants many seeds will have a bountiful harvest.
— *2 Corinthians 9:6*

Ten Thoughts to Ponder

1. Artificial memory is writing something down so we won't forget it.
2. With God's help, I can do more than I am capable of doing.
3. The most difficult thing about needing help is not knowing where I need help most.
4. If artificial intelligence could have a relationship with God, it could do more than it knows to do.
5. To avoid distractions, the first thing I need is to know that I am caught up in a distraction.
6. Looking for help where there is no help is an exercise in futility.
7. If we had any idea of God's glorious plan for us, we would immediately recognize our inability and would desperately cry out for his help.
8. Since I should never complain about the Lord's provision, I need to find a different label for all my complaints.
9. With all the things I am incapable of doing, I obviously need God's help. And then I need his help with all the things I am capable of doing.
10. I most need help when I'm thinking I don't need God's help.

Questions for Further Thought

- How can we prevent seeds of wickedness from taking root in our lives?
- What causes seeds of righteousness to grow?

Forbidden Fruit

Eve ate the forbidden fruit because she thought the serpent was right. Adam knew better, so he would have stopped her if he had been there when the serpent made the fruit look so good. Why was Eve deceived, but Adam was not?

Eve didn't know God as well as Adam did. She didn't know that God couldn't lie. She didn't know they both would die.

> *God ... cannot lie, nor can he do anything that later would be cause for repentance. When he makes a promise, you can be sure he will fulfill it. Whatever he says, he will do, always keeping his word.*
> — *Numbers 23:19*

Ten Thoughts to Ponder

1. My mind cannot remember what it has already dismissed as unimportant.
2. What matters to me might not really matter.
3. Confidence in my ability is nothing compared to confidence in God's ability when I have surrendered my desires to him.
4. When I think I know what I need to know, I don't know nearly enough.
5. If I think I can't, there's no chance that I can.
6. Because I know all things are possible with God, being told I can't do something entices me to prove it can be done.
7. Without God-confidence, I would have to believe the naysayers who say I am no good.
8. With each added word, a lengthy statement loses its ability to be profound.
9. I have no problem coming up with words. I just don't know which ones to keep and how to arrange what's left.
10. To avoid deceiving ourselves, we must question the truth to be sure it's true.

Questions for Further Thought

- Why do children sometimes burn themselves after being told the fire is hot?
- How can we be sure God cannot tell a lie?

Watchful Eye

On the right freeway lane, just going with the flow, I kept a watchful eye on the traffic to my left and behind me. Oh, no! Over the next hill, an eighteen-wheeler was stalled, blocking my lane. With no time to think, I jumped the curb, flew across the high shoulder, and never slowed down.

If I hadn't already known where the other traffic was, or if I had frozen in panic, I would have died for sure.

> *You should always be prepared, because you do not know when the Son of Man will come.*
> — *Matthew 25:13*

Ten Thoughts to Ponder

1. With the desire to make sense of what doesn't make sense, I can easily draw a conclusion that has no conclusive proof.
2. Without God's help, I am helpless beyond what I imagine.
3. Defining what I want without knowing what God wants is trying to profess what I don't know.
4. When it comes to ignorance, I consider myself the very best, which explains my dependency upon the Lord.
5. If God is behind Door 1, nothing behind Door 2 or 3 could be worthy of pursuit.
6. People who have always lived in bondage cannot imagine what it's like to be free.
7. To see God's glory, we must first believe.
8. If we don't recognize God in what we see, what we don't see will not reveal him to us.
9. I need God's help to do my part so he can do his part in fulfilling his purpose for my life.
10. "Distractions of desire" threaten to take us in a direction that will require God's redirection.

Questions for Further Thought

- In what ways can we prepare for danger that we don't know is coming?
- How have you coped with the thought that you might die?

Passing Grade

A week late getting back to school after Easter vacation, I had mostly forgotten or didn't care about what I'd learned in my first-period English class. I was given my final exam that would weigh heavily on my semester grade. I didn't know who the writers were, what they wrote, or why. On each essay question, I wildly guessed, thinking *any* answer had to be better than writing nothing.

I could hardly believe I scored 96, apparently for my imagination.

Blessed are those who persevere and pass the test.
— *James 1:12*

Ten Thoughts to Ponder

1. Before *we* can change our world, a great thought must first change *us*.
2. Confessing what we don't believe is the worst kind of hypocrisy.
3. God's prodding is not the kind of pain we need to avoid.
4. Wanting what others have is foolishness, because my position and purpose are not the same as anybody else. I need no more than what God wants me to have.
5. God loves us the way we are, but he has no plan to leave us the way we are.
6. God wanting none to perish explains why evil that is worse than Sodom and Gomorrah hasn't already been wiped out.
7. Fear of calamity and fear of Satan are best refocused to a fear of the Lord.
8. Saying I don't want to do what I am doing is an argument against reality.
9. Today is all we have to enjoy, since the past is over and the future isn't yet.
10. In our relationship with God, a faulty connection is the cause for having no power.

Questions for Further Thought

- Why is learning more important than making a good grade?
- How can we know what we most need to know so we can pass the Lord's tests that come without notice?

Purchase Price

A boy made a toy sailboat, lost it when the wind carried it down the river, and then saw it for sale in the window at the antique shop. He emptied every coin from his piggybank, went back to the store, and bought the boat.

"Little boat," he said, beaming, "now you're twice mine. I created you, and now I gave everything to make you mine forever."

> *You do not belong entirely to yourself, for you belong to God, purchased at great cost. Therefore, glorify God in body and spirit, which both belong to him. God paid a high price for you, so your highest obligation is to serve him above the needs of men.*
> — *1 Corinthians 6:19–20; 7:23*

Ten Thoughts to Ponder

1. Walking with God means I don't have to plan my direction.
2. The commandment to have no other gods says God is jealous, wanting to be idolized above anyone or anything else.
3. The absence of something is difficult to observe.
4. In lying to myself, I must believe what I say, not what I do.
5. Knowing the truth will help me only if I *embrace* the transformation God wants for me. The devils believe and tremble, but they will never change.
6. Infatuation is good only when we are infatuated by the right infatuation, which is walking with God.
7. God's prescriptions are the very best medicine.
8. In trusting the Lord, I surrender my desire to be in control.
9. Without faith, I cannot trust the Lord.
10. The extent of our effort exposes the truth about our desire.

Questions for Further Thought

- Why have some Christians completely surrendered their lives and possessions to please the Lord, yet others want to hold something back for themselves?
- To what extent should we believe what Jesus said—that we are blessed more by giving than by getting?

Changing Direction

To avoid the land where he was told to go, Jonah took a ship out to sea. When a violent storm threatened to drown everyone on board, he saw how hard it was to escape the Lord's call. Many others have changed direction to go the Lord's way.

On the road to Damascus, Saul saw the light and could no longer resist the Lord's prodding.

> *You are a chosen people of the royal order, a pure and holy multitude in a unique position to exalt the one who has brought you out of darkness into his marvelous light.*
> — *1 Peter 2:9*

Ten Thoughts to Ponder

1. Direction without motivation is a sailboat on a sea without wind.
2. Confession has value only when it leads to permanent change for the better.
3. "Weird" is a wonderful condition when it's what God wants.
4. The popular name for baloney is hot dog.
5. There must always be more to be and do, or hope in life is lost.
6. Giving up or not giving up can be either a great gain or a great loss. Without the Lord's direction, I can't distinguish the difference.
7. Pursuit requires no more than relentless steps in the right direction.
8. Needing God's help may come as a surprise to us, but it's never a surprise to God.
9. To be the person God wants me to be, I cannot be the person I used to be, and I cannot be the person I am right now. I must change.
10. Without desire, intensity of focus is a far-fetched dream.

Questions for Further Thought

- What happened to turn you from darkness to light?
- What motivates people to run away from the Lord?

Expiration Date

At the age of twelve, I thought a grownup was anyone old enough to drive. I had read that the average man lived almost seventy years, which was too far away to be of any concern. But at age thirty, I anticipated meeting my Maker.

Not knowing when the Lord would come for me, I decided to always be ready to go to him.

> *If you are ready for the Lord's coming, you don't have to worry about when it will happen. You know perfectly well that the day of the Lord will come unexpectedly, as a thief in the night.*
> *— 1 Thessalonians 5:1–2*

Ten Thoughts to Ponder

1. I can't be satisfied until I know God is satisfied with me.
2. When we are entirely God-centered, we are rich beyond measure, no matter how much or how little we have.
3. In hoping for the wrong things, we lead hopeless lives.
4. If we knew God's perspective, we would be shocked at how drastically it differs from the common worldview.
5. Because of our free will, we hold power over God to either restrict or surrender to whatever he wants to work through us.
6. The wonder and the glory of God's presence is our privilege in being eager participants.
7. All things considered, everything God does and everything he doesn't do is exactly what he chooses to do.
8. There is no science, philosophy, or doctrine that can establish truth different from what God says is true.
9. Questions have no value if they don't lead to spiritual awareness and helpful answers.
10. Determination is constructive if it is God-inspired, but if self-directed, determination is destructive.

Questions for Further Thought

- How can we prepare for the unexpected?
- If you knew the day when the Lord was taking you to Heaven, what might you do differently right now?

Worry Wart

Supposedly, over 90 percent of what people worry about never happens. But so many things *could* go wrong. What could I do?

Because so many things were beyond my control, I had to learn that the best way to get what I wanted was to want what I got.

> *Your Father in Heaven causes the sun to rise on the evil as well as the good. He sends rain on both the righteous and unrighteous. You should show kindness as he does.*
> — *Matthew 5:45*

Ten Thoughts to Ponder
1. Tools that save time give us much more work than we have time to do.
2. I cannot know my perception of reality is real when it is no more than a perception.
3. I don't need to be concerned about what God hasn't done—unless there's something I need to do to make that possible.
4. I want to embrace the truth, not what I would *like* to be true—but for that, I need God's help.
5. Inflation helps us believe we have more when we really have less.
6. The other things I need to be doing may be necessary to prepare me for what I need to be doing.
7. If God knows the numbers of hairs on my head, his knowledge of me is beyond my understanding.
8. Nothing is more impossible than knowing what I don't know.
9. Worries are a waste of energy when I can do nothing about what I am worried about.
10. Self-centeredness is okay as long as it follows the way God is self-centered, where our nature is to give, not get.

Questions for Further Thought

- Why do people worry about so many things that they can't control?
- What kinds of things should people be worried about, but often aren't?

Heaven Can Wait

The Sunday school teacher was shocked when little Johnny said he didn't want to go to Heaven. "Really?" she said. "Do you want to spend eternity in Hell?"

"Oh, no," he said. "I thought you was gettin' up a busload now."

Who do I want besides you? In the realm above and the earth below, your presence with me is more important than anything else.
— *Psalm 73:25*

Ten Thoughts to Ponder

1. The obvious isn't really obvious when we have missed seeing the obvious.
2. Having my way can never be as good as having God's way.
3. Because of what I don't know, what I imagine is certainly by no means certain.
4. When we feel like we are in complete control, only a willingness to accept the truth will reveal how little control we actually have.
5. Houses built upon an unshakable foundation are safe and secure until an earthquake proves otherwise.
6. Practicing the presence of God helps us sense God's presence for the rest of the day.
7. Desire that is beyond my ability is a waste of energy unless I can find help.
8. My ability to plan is dependent upon an unpredictable future.
9. Artificial intelligence thinks I would say what I would never even think, let alone say.
10. To do wrong, we need only to close our eyes to what we know is right.

Questions for Further Thought

- What can we do to make our walk on Earth more like Heaven and less like Hell?
- If you knew you were leaving Earth in three months, what things would suddenly become more important? What would become unimportant?

Lame Excuses

I didn't have time. I lacked ability. I didn't know how. I could do it later. It wasn't my responsibility. Somebody else was more capable.

My mother ruined my great skill at making excuses to avoid what I didn't want to do. "Where there's a will," she said, "there's a way."

> *The hour arrived when everyone should come. He sent his servant to tell them, "Come, for everything is now ready." One after another, they made excuses.*
> *— Luke 3:17–18*

Ten Thoughts to Ponder

1. No matter how good things are, I can choose to be disappointed, since they can be better. No matter how bad things are, I can choose to be thrilled, since they can be worse.
2. If I have nothing but what has been provided from above, a thief is in trouble for stealing from God, not me.
3. If God holds the advantage in a battle, he is on the side that appears to be winning.
4. Help for my ignorance is as much a matter of being and doing as it is learning and knowing.
5. Since God is my life, for a better life, I need more of God.
6. When I am not sure where I am and where to go, I most need God's Positioning System, which might be more expensive than any other GPS.
7. People risk losing their dependence upon the Lord when they fail to recognize that he alone can satisfy their needs.
8. The Lord's purpose is immeasurably better than ours, because his work has *eternal* value.
9. The joke is on us if we think we can win an argument with God.
10. Mistakes should be admitted for what they are, because excuses don't help.

Questions for Further Thought

- What do people accomplish by making excuses?
- When have you made an excuse that didn't work? Why?

Misplaced Respect

On Sunday evening, sister Mary Margaret gave her usual testimony. She had been under satanic attack all week, but thankfully, she had survived. "Bless his holy name," she said.

I had to wonder why she gave Satan so much respect.

> *Completely surrender your will to whatever God wants. Then your resistance to the devil is an absolute no, and he has no reason to hang around.*
> — *James 4:7*

Ten Thoughts to Ponder

1. Foolishness is making comparisons without true, accurate, and complete information.
2. Without exception, self-imposed rules lose their value with the first exception.
3. If we want to learn, we should listen to everything the Great Teacher has to say.
4. Fiction becomes nonfiction when it holds life-changing truth.
5. No matter who I am today, I can be better tomorrow—but not until tomorrow arrives. So I need to work on today.
6. Hope in Christ is much more than wishful thinking.
7. A selfie can't picture the needs of others.
8. A law that allows exceptions is nothing more than a suggestion.
9. Comparisons are meaningless if they don't encourage improvements.
10. All who know the Lord have experienced miracles they don't know about.

Questions for Further Thought

- If Satan is like a roaring lion, seeking whom he might devour, for what reasons should Christians have no fear?
- Given the fact that Satan is a fallen angel, able to be in only one place among billions of people on this very large planet, who is the "enemy" able to make individuals feel like they are under constant attack?

My GPS

God wants to be my GPS (God's Positioning System). So far, he's not been willing to be my chauffeur. I still have to do the driving.

Like a GPS, God recalculates. I can still go my own way, but I need to be careful. He might guide me to where he doesn't want me to go. Would he really do that? Yes, just ask Balaam. My best choice is to go wherever he wants, and he will take me the right way.

> *The steps of righteous people are directed by the Lord, and they love to walk with him. They may stumble, but they won't fall flat, because God will help them up.*
> — *Psalm 37:23–24*

Ten Thoughts to Ponder
1. *Self-corrected ignorance* is a conflict in terms.
2. Imitations are excuses for reality.
3. People who don't want to discover God must have a desire not to see the obvious.
4. Artificial intelligence can appear to be stupid, because it doesn't know what it doesn't know.
5. Apart from what I might know from the Lord, my intelligence is immeasurably close to nothing.
6. Excuses are an escape from the reality we know but don't want to admit.
7. A forest will grow from planting seeds.
8. To meet my needs, God sometimes gives me what I don't want.
9. To avoid being an obstacle to what God wants, I must want everything he wants.
10. If he sees every sparrow that falls, nothing can be trivial with God.

Questions for Further Thought
- Why might people think they can't trust directions from a GPS?
- What keeps people from believing they can trust God's guidance?

Careful with Words

My parents were Bible college graduates who insisted on correct grammar at home, which helped me make good grades in my English classes. Grampa saying, "Ain't," was okay, but I couldn't say that.

Our Father God has a high standard for the words we use.

> *You can be sure, on Judgment Day, people will have to account for every word carelessly spoken. By your words, you will be either justified or condemned.*
> — *Matthew 12:36–37*

Ten Thoughts to Ponder

1. In following the Lord, stopping points can be no more than resting points that launch us forward.
2. Nothing can be more destructive than wanting something God doesn't want.
3. Human logic is far too limited for us to comprehend the infinite dimensions of God.
4. Speculation upon possibilities can be a necessary first step to discover undeniable truth, but only if we *want* to know the truth.
5. When we tell God we can't do what he wants, we fool ourselves, because he knows, with his help, all things are possible.
6. As long as I can give an excuse that I think is reasonable, I don't have to change my behavior.
7. The pursuit of knowledge is a dangerous distraction if it doesn't support God's purpose in what we are doing.
8. Focus on the target isn't as good as focusing on dead center.
9. Seeking the Lord is like panning for gold. We can never get enough.
10. Excuses make us feel better about not doing what we know we should do.

Questions for Further Thought

- Why do people say what they soon wish they hadn't said?
- What must we do for the Holy Spirit to give us the right words?

Lost and Found

After a wonderful time at church on Sunday evening, my wife and I were out to dinner, visiting with friends. Where was our three-year-old son? Neither of us could remember seeing him recently.

The church was locked and dark when we found him, sleeping under the pew where we had been sitting. Now I know how Mary and Joseph so easily lost the Son of God.

After three days, [Joseph and Mary] found [Jesus] in the Temple, sitting among the teachers, listening and asking questions.
— Luke 2:46

Ten Thoughts to Ponder

1. Artificial intelligence can explain its ignorance only by blaming its creators for making it what it is.
2. The more irons we have in the fire, the more places we must make for our irons.
3. Our three great discoveries in life: that God has an important use for us, what he wants us to do, and finally, how to do it.
4. Ignorance is based on my feeling of stupidity, but given how ignorant I am, I might be entirely wrong.
5. We need God for solutions because he knows the problem better than we can even guess.
6. Any waste of my time loses an important moment to accomplish something worthwhile.
7. If I can find a way to enjoy what I must do, I can have a much better time doing it.
8. With an excuse, we avoid the truth that others know about us.
9. On my own, I might try, but I must have the Lord's help for the doing of it.
10. Reality becomes relevant only when we believe it.

Questions for Further Thought

- How can we comfort parents who have lost a child? How can we find comfort for our own losses?
- When has what you have gained been worth much more than what you have lost?

Wrong Solution

Back when kids could park under a shade tree and do car repairs, I replaced the spark plugs on my 1954 Chevy. Why wasn't the car running better? The fuel pump wasn't working properly.

Finding the right solution in life can be difficult without the Lord's help to identify what our problems really are.

When we think we know the answer, we're unaware of what we have missed.
— 1 Corinthians 8:2

Ten Thoughts to Ponder

1. To be the "me" that God wants me to be, I cannot be the "me" that I have been.
2. To shorten the distance between us and God, we must move in his direction.
3. Fighting the imagined problem has absolutely no power to defeat the real problem.
4. A $10 success is better than a $10,000 disappointment.
5. Jesus is the author and finisher of our faith because he is the Word we choose to believe.
6. Our treasures are whatever we choose to value most.
7. Without the Holy Spirit and a sincere heart, religion is *artificial* worship.
8. Encouragement is a helpful boost of energy, but only when I can see improvement.
9. *Wanting* inspiration is the first step in looking. *Seeking* inspiration is the first step in finding. *Finding* inspiration is the first step in writing to inspire others.
10. Excuses are most easily believed by those who make the excuses.

Questions for Further Thought

- Why do problems that seem to have obvious solutions sometimes turn out to be wrong?
- When the wrong way looks right and the right way looks wrong, how can we be sure we've made the best choice?

Digging Down

Pointing to the opposite side of the globe, my kindergarten teacher said, "Dig a hole straight down, and you'll be in China."

I shared my discovery with a friend, who said, "How far down do we have to dig?" The globe was just a few feet across. Using tablespoons from the kitchen, we tried but didn't get very far before it was too dark to see. My friend got a flashlight, hoping to see how close we might be.

> *Miners carry lamps into the darkness, digging deep as they search for earth's treasures.*
> — *Job 28:3*

Ten Thoughts to Ponder

1. Attention paid to the wrong things makes it impossible to say the right things.
2. While worried about future steps, I can miss taking the next right step.
3. If I'm not bothered by what I can't change, then I can enjoy the bother about what I most need to do.
4. Some people keep valuables in a safe where, for lack of use, they have no value.
5. Spiritual listening is doing what I need to do instead of what I want to do.
6. God will give us the ability to do more than we can imagine—if we prefer his way above ours.
7. If you don't believe in the reward, you won't do the work.
8. My initiative has value only when it satisfies God's purpose.
9. The greatest obstacle to learning is assuming that we know.
10. In trying to hear what I *expect* God to say, I can miss what he is *actually* saying.

Questions for Further Thought

- For how long should we dig into God's Word to discover his truth?
- What kinds of treasures are most worthy of pursuit? Why might we know what they are, but still not pursue them?

Apology Accepted

My heart skipped a beat when I saw the red and blue flashing lights behind me and pulled over to the curb. What had I done wrong?

The police officer walked up, glanced at my windshield, and waited for me to lower my window. "I'm sorry," he said. "I thought your inspection sticker had expired.

I was so thankful to be caught for doing something right.

> *You do well when you endure pain and suffering to do what is right.*
> *You deserve no recognition when you suffer for doing wrong, but if you*
> *patiently endure pain in doing good, God is well pleased.*
> — *1 Peter 2:19–20*

Ten Thoughts to Ponder

1. Spiritual listening is doing what I need to do instead of what I want to do.
2. If I value the giver more than the gift, then I must be concerned that my use of the gift pleases the giver.
3. With God's help, I can do what I don't know how to do.
4. Walking with the Lord requires one step at a time, in whatever direction he chooses to go.
5. I need more and more and more and more of God. And then I still need more.
6. When we need an attitude adjustment, we do well to seek help from the Lord.
7. Recognizing my need for God's help is the first step toward getting the help I need most.
8. Concern for things beyond my control is a waste of mental and emotional energy.
9. Improvement cannot happen without some kind of change.
10. Truth that will be misunderstood is better left unsaid.

Questions for Further Thought

- Why do people hide their "skeletons" in closets when both they and God know they are there?
- Given the wonderful feeling that comes from knowing we've pleased the Lord, why would people want to do anything else?

Mistaken Identity

To get Charlie's attention, you had to use his new name. He had the uniform, provided by the asylum workers to keep him from screaming. When he heard his name, he turned and stood with the perfect pose, the same as the famous picture of him.

Charlie hated who he had been, so he thought he'd do better as Napoleon.

> *Beloved, we may be God's children, but we don't yet know what we will become. But the more of him we see, the more we'll want to be like him, for we shall see how great he really is.*
> *— 1 John 3:2*

Ten Thoughts to Ponder

1. Being mindful of the right things requires my acquiring, to some degree, the mind of Christ.
2. More than from prayer about my needs, I benefit most from open and honest conversation with the Lord about my interests and concerns.
3. As I surrender more to the Lord, I have more confidence.
4. The creative nature of God can't be boring. Ask the platypus.
5. A process isn't effective when a step has been overlooked.
6. Depending on a weekend church service for the spiritual energy needed for the week is like expecting an electric car to make it from California to New York on a single charge.
7. What we believe will not change the truth, but it will change what we say and do.
8. Turning up the sound doesn't improve the message.
9. I can chew gum while walking, but I can't listen and talk at the same time.
10. If God will help me improve, then I will have "helpful improvement," which is so much better than trying to improve on my own.

Questions for Further Thought

- If we're not happy with who we are, how can we become the person we want to be?
- How might our desire differ from who God wants us to be?

Something or Nothing

Miss Armstrong's fifth-grade class wasn't listening. She felt like a babysitter because the kids didn't care about learning.

One day, thinking something had to be better than nothing, she asked what the kids wanted to learn. When allowed to pursue what they felt they needed, all the students became eager to learn.

You will experience times when people reject sound teaching for what suits their desires. They will love those who preach what they want to hear.
— 2 Timothy 4:3

Ten Thoughts to Ponder

1. For my mind to be sharp, I need the Lord's help because I don't know how to sharpen it.
2. As I walk with the Lord, wholeheartedly seeking his direction, every day gets better. It just doesn't always seem that way, because God needs time for the bad days to work for good.
3. Without spiritual sensitivity, we can think God is nowhere around when he sees every action and knows our thoughts.
4. I need to spend less time on trivial things so I can spend more time on what's important.
5. If what needs to be shaken isn't shaken, we risk building upon an unreliable foundation.
6. My greatest concern is my lack of concern for what I need.
7. Since God created humans in his image, there are significant similarities between who God is and who we are meant to be.
8. Having confidence in God, we anticipate the good he will do—but it's not a problem if he does something different.
9. Having all the dots doesn't help me if I don't know how to connect them.
10. Big software companies might show little interest in helping me. God is bigger than any enterprise on Earth, yet he is always sensitive to anything that bothers me.

Questions for Further Thought

- Why do people say ignorance is bliss?
- What lesson caused a significant turn in your life?

Reading Signs

On my early-morning drive to work, the fog was a thick, white blanket. In the darkness I couldn't see the freeway signs until I was a few feet away. The sixty-mile-per-hour speed limit was meaningless, because I couldn't see well enough to drive more than ten.

Wait! I almost missed my turn. After a few blocks, I saw strange landmarks beyond the streetlight and knew I was lost.

You can look at the sky and predict the weather, but you cannot interpret the signs of the times.
— Matthew 16:3

Ten Thoughts to Ponder

1. God's help is meaningless without my willingness to do what he wants.
2. If we who have grandchildren don't want any to perish, God must be devasted when his children forsake him.
3. Self-appraisal has to be based in one direction or the other.
4. Depending on the desire to improve, relentless practice will make us either better or worse.
5. Prospecting for what we want is like fishing all day on the wrong side of the boat.
6. Taking one step at a time with the Lord is my only choice, since I can't make it on my own and I don't know the details of God's plan.
7. If we expect to enjoy the fullness of God's presence, we had better be whatever God wants us to be.
8. My God-confidence soars with the doing, not just the knowing.
9. Like sensing how hot fire is, which is impossible at a distance, spiritual sensitivity requires being close to the Lord.
10. Hope has no value if we can never have what we hope for.

Questions for Further Thought

- Why do people sometimes miss obvious signs?
- What reasons might we have to think we know something that God doesn't know?

Dreaming Big

On Christmas Eve 1950, I skipped the black-and-white newsprint Montgomery Ward catalog pages and found the glossy color pictures of toys I knew were too expensive.

I learned to say thank you for the clothes I needed and not to show disappointment when I didn't get what I wanted. Perhaps that day would come.

I could still dream.

> *Hard-working farmers will have plenty to eat, but those who only dream of a harvest lack good sense. Without vision, people perish, but only by following God's direction can we guarantee success.*
> — *Proverbs 12:11; 29:18*

Ten Thoughts to Ponder
1. *Thinking* I can't. That's all I need to make myself incapable.
2. Not knowing I am lost is worse than knowing I am lost.
3. Due to a programmer's lack of intelligence, Artificial Intelligence can look really stupid.
4. Without the Holy Spirit to guide me, I will continue to believe the lie that I am sure is the truth.
5. My willingness to do more for the Lord helps him do more for me.
6. Reality is invisible when we don't want to see it.
7. The last inch might as well be a mile if I don't have God's help in getting there.
8. I didn't know I was lost until I discovered that I wasn't where I thought I was.
9. From the top of the mountain, I could see for miles until the fog kept me from seeing anything but clouds.
10. Without knowing for sure what's in the bag, we should not buy "a pig in a poke."

Questions for Further Thought
- How can we tell the difference between dreams born out of our own imaginations and what might be from the Lord?
- In what ways might our dreams reflect our concerns?

Puzzling Pieces

I loved putting together picture puzzles. I quickly learned about color and shape. Pieces with a straight side belonged along the edge. With adjacent straight sides, the piece went on a corner. Light blue and white made up the sky, and other colors formed the landscape. An interlocking edge on one piece wouldn't fit unless the shape precisely complemented another piece.

If only the puzzles of life would fit together as easily.

> *Those who know and respect the Lord will treasure their relationship with him, a mystery that others cannot figure out.*
> — *Psalm 25:14*

Ten Thoughts to Ponder

1. By finding pleasure in the choices I should make, I am more likely to make the right choices.
2. Without God's guidance, I may think I see clearly when I am actually lost in the fog.
3. To know the truth about myself, I need to know what God knows.
4. If I can give up on the trivial things, I can move on to other more-important things.
5. I don't have to worry about what doesn't need to be fixed, because whatever is left is the problem.
6. If all things work for good, fulfilling God's purpose in my life, then I must be making progress, even if I can't see it.
7. When people don't care enough about God, they think God doesn't care enough about them.
8. If I am looking for *easy*, I'm not likely to find *effective*.
9. With human free will, God has created an exceptional challenge for himself, even with all his power.
10. A prospector refuses to quit believing gold will be found, even though it hasn't yet been seen.

Questions for Further Thought

- What steps are most important in solving a mystery?
- How can we understand more about God?

God's Miracle

Coincidences happen every day, but sometimes I wonder if God has intervened. When the results can't be a coincidence, I must recognize God's hand at work.

I have a miracle testimony, not for what I have but for how he took worthless me and made something of value.

I'm God's amazing miracle because he's causing me to be like him.

Like someone looking into a mirror, we see the beauty of who we will become, more and more like the Lord, being changed from glory to even greater glory by the work of his Spirit.
— 2 Corinthians 2:18

Ten Thoughts to Ponder
1. Truth doesn't need an argument to make it true.
2. Idiocy is accepting a religious substitute for the reality of God's presence.
3. For God's light to shine through us, we must first be eager receptors of his light.
4. When God's goal becomes my goal, fulfillment is inevitable, provided I don't give up on his eternal plan.
5. If I fail to recognize my total dependence upon the Lord, I'll have to be taught that lesson again.
6. The price God paid should tell us how valuable we are to him.
7. Wishing is a waste of energy if nothing can be done and a waste of time if something can be done and I'm not doing it.
8. Softening our hard hearts is a difficult, time-consuming task, even for the Lord.
9. To change the things I cannot change, God is my only hope.
10. To destroy the value of progress, all I have to do is give up.

Questions for Further Thought

- What is the best definition of a "miracle"?
- Throughout all of biblical history, what do you think are the top three greatest miracles?

Leap of Faith

As a young teenager, I jumped off the roof to see if an umbrella would work like a parachute. Don't laugh. It didn't work for me like it did for Mary Poppins. My umbrella collapsed upward and left me speeding to the ground like a rock.

I didn't bounce, but I rolled, dusted myself off, and knew I wouldn't try that again.

The steps of righteous people are directed by the Lord, and they love to walk with him. They may stumble, but they won't fall flat, because God will help them up.
— *Psalm 37:23–24*

Ten Thoughts to Ponder

1. God's promise to give us the desires of our heart can be fatal if those desires aren't what he wants.
2. Our comfort zone can be a burial casket.
3. Profession of ignorance is the first step toward understanding truth.
4. Praising God is a launching pad for achieving excellence.
5. Following the Lord isn't easy, but it's better and easier than getting him to follow me.
6. Having what God wants requires an adjustment in what I want.
7. To think "outside the box," I must leave my comfort zone.
8. Artificial intelligence can't discover God, because its programmers can't tell it how.
9. I need God's help to accept the way things need to be so I can let go of my desire for the way things don't need to be.
10. Failure is a fresh opportunity to surrender to the Lord's will.

Questions for Further Thought

- When would it be stupidity to take a leap of faith, and when might it be the smartest thing we could do?
- How do we know our faith is well-placed in God and not in some fantasy that we believe is true?

Legal Immigrant

Many jokes refer to the pearly gates and entering Heaven. But if I don't meet the citizenship requirements, I won't be laughing.

Admission is far from free. Besides the price Jesus paid, I must become a "new creature," changed to who God wants me to be.

> *Your self-serving nature ... sexual impurity ... anger ... envy ... preying upon others ... mindless partying ... don't think for a second that you can do such things and have any place in the Kingdom of God.*
> — *Galatians 5:19–21*

Ten Thoughts to Ponder

1. Without God's guidance, I can stumble over truth, believing it is a lie.
2. When people don't know God, they have no reason to respect who he is.
3. One of the best signs of improvement is making better choices.
4. Hoping for a *better* past is an argument against reality, and so is a *forgiven* past if we can't accept God's forgiveness and become who he wants us to be.
5. Having the utmost respect for my father, I would never do anything that might displease him.
6. Believing a lie is attempted suicide, but the truth brings life.
7. Without God's help, I'm left sitting on the ground, unable to reach the moon, even though I can see it.
8. Wishing is a tragic excuse for not doing all we can do.
9. I can run through a troop and leap over a wall, but not without God's strength that enables me to do what he wants.
10. To be sure of God's truth, I must constantly question my truth, just in case it might be a little out of focus—or wrong, and I don't know it.

Questions for Further Thought

- What conditions must be met for us to be content with where we are and not want to be somewhere else?
- What does it mean to be *in* the world but not *of* the world?

Having My Way

I heard the preacher say, "Where you go doesn't matter. God will go with you, no matter what direction you choose."

Bad idea, I thought. If I could talk to Jonah, I'd hear firsthand what it's like to go my own way. As best I can, I choose to follow the Lord in whatever direction he wants to go.

> *Those who abandon your lovingkindness are grasping at something that can't save them. With a sacrifice of praise, I will keep my commitment to you, for you are my salvation.*
> — *John 2:8–9*

Ten Thoughts to Ponder

1. Apart from God, striving for excellence can make us worthless.
2. We can *know* God without having to *understand* or *define* him.
3. Transparency requires being open and honest, first with ourselves, then with God.
4. An endless journey requires eternity for its completion, no matter how fast or slow we travel.
5. How easily I can make an observation, but with great difficulty I will determine whether that observation is correct.
6. Woe to those who are comfortable with their sin, for they are in bad trouble.
7. The ultimate disregard for authority is to ignore what God would have us do.
8. *Improvement* is good, but in our persistent work with the Lord, *achievement* is the greater reward.
9. I know when I think I know, but I might not really know.
10. God will allow me to take a wrong step when it's needed to recognize the right step.

Questions for Further Thought

- Why do people think going their own way is better than following the Lord?
- What must we do or what must happen before we can appreciate the value of God's plan for us?

Truth Revealed

I think I know the truth, but is it *really* the truth? Or do I just *think* it's true. How can I know for sure?

I wonder how the Pharisees felt when Jesus said they'd be free when they knew the truth.

Jesus said, "If you keep following what I say, you really are my disciples. And you will know the truth, and the truth will set you free. When he, the Spirit of truth, comes, he will guide you into all the truth. He will not speak on his own; he will speak only what he hears, and he will tell you what is yet to come."
— *John 8:31–32; 16:13*

Ten Thoughts to Ponder

1. Without death and burial, there can be no resurrection life.
2. What I know is what I know—but only if God helps me know—because otherwise, I'm not sure I know.
3. The extent of his love will not allow God to be self-centered.
4. All of eternity won't be long enough for God to teach me everything he knows.
5. Selfish pride can have no part in *genuine* praise for who God is.
6. If God will show me what to do and then help me do it, I can enjoy the reward for our having done it.
7. God's miracles aren't limited to what we believe is possible.
8. In seeing the obvious, we can miss seeing the not-so-obvious that is more important.
9. I am thankful that God wants to be found. Otherwise, I could never find him.
10. A goose can boast for as long as he isn't cooked.

Questions for Further Thought

- What makes Jesus' truth so disturbing that it is impossible for some people to accept?
- How can we distinguish the truth found in Scripture from the popular interpretations that might not be true?

Foolishness

My dad said I needed three lies to cover the first one, nine lies to cover the next three, and twenty-seven to cover the last nine. I'd soon be lost trying to remember them all. Before he told me, I lived in ignorance. But after I knew, telling a lie would be foolish.

A fool lies about God's existence, not because of ignorance but because he knows better.

> *Only a fool would say in his heart,* There is no God. *Their thinking is warped in self-deceit, because they love their sin and don't want to do what is right.*
> — *Psalm 14:1*

Ten Thoughts to Ponder

1. As we live in God's presence, we can anticipate much greater pleasures as we experience more of God's presence.
2. Standing calmly in the midst of the storm requires peace that defies understanding.
3. The greatest of all prayers in Scripture is to ask God for his will, not ours.
4. The feeling of success can be a useful force in moving toward the reality of success—if the feeling is real.
5. Our conscious action when facing tragedy is more important that our thoughtless reaction.
6. Saying "God is love" is almost meaningless when we liken our human perception of love to God's indescribable love.
7. What we value most can best be measured by how we spend our time, effort, and money.
8. To understand God's truth, we must distinguish the difference between reality and religion.
9. God's love is all about helping others, not ourselves.
10. No matter how much we might dislike the truth, there is no reasonable alternative—unless we want to believe a lie.

Questions for Further Thought

- What might motivate people to lie to themselves?
- How are mistakes different from accidents?

Dry Well

Divorced from five husbands and now living with a sixth man, the woman Jesus met at Sychar must have been searching for satisfaction for a long time.

Jesus fills the void in our lives, which nothing else can satisfy.

Those who drink the water I give will never become thirsty. My water is a fresh artesian spring, bubbling with everlasting life.
— *John 4:14*

Ten Thoughts to Ponder

1. Satan as "an angel of light" offers to satisfy what we want as opposed to the much greater glory of having what God wants.
2. With the Lord directing our steps, what we experience may look bad, but it must work for good.
3. We never quit growing until we start dying, which says our growth in Christ must continue forever.
4. We can meet all the conditions for learning, yet we still need God's guidance to know if what we've learned is right.
5. In making a purchase, we must believe that the value of what we will receive is greater than the value of what we give up.
6. We believe a lie if we think we can have something for nothing. There is always a cost.
7. Humor can be disarming, allowing subtle truths and lies to slip in, unnoticed.
8. God gave his priceless life so I could give up my worthless life to spend eternity with him.
9. With the Lord, since even the worst times cannot end in defeat, the best of times is inevitable.
10. No matter how much I have, if I'm not content with what I have, I can feel like I'm living in poverty.

Questions for Further Thought

- When looking for satisfaction in life, why do people look in all the wrong places?
- How can we be like King David, who praised the Lord because his cup was full and overflowing?

Time for God

The preacher said, "You need to make time for God."

Great idea. How many minutes should that be? I decided every minute of the day should belong to God.

The time can't be only quiet-time prayer, because the doing is as important as the listening.

> *Anyone who hears my words but never acts on them is like a foolish man who built his house on sand, without a foundation.*
> — *Matthew 7:26*

Ten Thoughts to Ponder
1. People who blame Satan for their plight have identified the wrong enemy.
2. To do the right thing, we must give up doing the wrong thing.
3. We shouldn't count numbers, because sometimes God wants us to reach a multitude of one.
4. Given our self-centeredness, obvious lessons can be the most difficult to learn and remember.
5. If God doesn't lead me, I don't know when to speak up and when to shut up.
6. If we understand the value of God's light, we will never hesitate to radiate his light when we stand in the darkness.
7. When my desire matches what God desires, obedience is much easier, because he helps me overcome the obstacles.
8. Our opinion becomes our truth when we believe it and won't listen to any opposing opinion.
9. To have a loving nature like God, my personality must change to be like him.
10. We tend to become like the person we idolize, which is a good reason for intense worship of God.

Questions for Further Thought

- What does the way you spend your time say about what you treasure most?
- What does it mean to "pray without ceasing"?

Namesake

In school, I had nicknames like Odd Ball, Frankfurter, and Red. Some teachers called me "special," "smart," and "gifted," but one teacher called me "stupid."

The biblical characters Abram, Simon, and Saul became Abraham, Peter, and Paul. Because of his self-sacrificing service, Jesus earned a name above every other name.

If you want the highest place of honor, you must be the best servant, just like the Son of Man, who has come to serve and sacrifice his life for many.
— *Matthew 20:27–28*

Ten Thoughts to Ponder

1. When I surrender my life to God, I give up a great present value to acquire something of eternal value, but only if I believe in the greater value.
2. Silence isn't golden when God would have us say something.
3. Without God's help, excellence is an impossible dream.
4. The difference between God and god is who or what we worship.
5. Tragic waste is any life that isn't surrendered to God's will.
6. Talking about getting help isn't much help.
7. Without his strength, I can't fulfill God's purpose for my life.
8. I get the most help when I'm doing what God wants me to do, because that's when I most need help.
9. In the fullness of God's nature, we will lose the ability to believe a lie.
10. For better growth and bearing more fruit, pruning in our lives is often necessary.

Questions for Further Thought

- Why might saying "in the name of Jesus" have no power?
- What makes the world's perception of greatness so different from the Kingdom of God?

Out of Sight

While playing hide-and-seek with my two-year-old granddaughter, I saw her curly hair and knew exactly where she was. She giggled, thinking I couldn't see her.

Might I think God can't see me, just because I don't see him? No, I'm old enough now to understand that not seeing God doesn't keep him from seeing me.

Lord, you have thoroughly examined me and know everything about me. You see every time I sit or stand. No matter how distant I might think I am, you still know my thoughts.
— Psalm 139:1–2

Ten Thoughts to Ponder

1. God's glory is found in our doing his will, because believing without the doing is worthless.
2. We should appreciate God's miracles because they pave the way for even greater miracles.
3. If we could describe the indescribable and define the undefinable, we could draw a precise picture of God.
4. To accomplish whatever God wants, I must surrender my desires to his guidance.
5. In our walk with the Lord, what goes without saying needs to be said.
6. God's appointments for today can't wait until tomorrow.
7. The greatest injustice of all injustices is failure to love God after he loved us so much.
8. Compared to eternity, a hundred billion years is less than a second.
9. God's eternal purpose has no time constraints.
10. If I can be guided by God's presence in all the small things, then the difficult choices won't be as difficult.

Questions for Further Thought

- If God sees everything we do and even knows our thoughts, how can we imagine getting away with anything?
- If God forgives us, what's the danger if we keep on sinning?

The Lord's Supper

Sitting in a Mexican restaurant today, Jesus might say, "Every time you grab a chip, remember my body that was given for you. When you dip the salsa, remember my blood that was shed for you."

Why might we think that? Because Jesus was encouraging his disciples to *remember* him, not create a religious form. So when you glance at your watch, remember your time on Earth is short.

This is my body that is given for you. Do this to remember me.
— *Luke 22:19*

Ten Thoughts to Ponder

1. Without God's intervention, all things could never work out for good, because all good things come from above.
2. Being self-made is *nothing* to boast about, because that would be *nothing* compared to what God could have done.
3. The difference between putty and granite is the willingness to change.
4. If a buy-one-get-one-free deal looks good, we should never miss a chance to exchange what we want for what God wants.
5. Unlike money that can be saved, time must be spent wisely or foolishly wasted.
6. In an emergency, our first call will be the one we believe will be the best help.
7. Humility is recognizing God's greatness and our smallness, not having a deflated ego.
8. Like with Abraham, our reliable GPS is following God's Promise Strategy.
9. Everybody's brain waves are different from everybody else on Earth, like a unique IP address that provides an exclusive connection with God—if we'll keep it activated.
10. Talking to myself is wonderful because I have a captive audience who will usually agree with me. But not always.

Questions for Further Thought

- Why are we told to remember what Jesus did for us?
- How can you best remember what you don't want to forget?

Happy Holidays

Those who oppose Easter and Christmas celebrations haven't escaped the truth by wishing people a happy holiday.

For the day to be *happy*, we need the Lord. And *holidays* is a word from the old English *haligdæg*, meaning "holy days" or "set apart for God."

> *One man treats some days as being holy, while another person believes every day belongs to the Lord. Let each person be convinced in his own mind and behave accordingly.*
> — *Romans 14:5*

Ten Thoughts to Ponder

1. Without a reason to think I will be successful, having a goal isn't much help.
2. Pain and suffering have great value when the experience brings us closer to God.
3. When we have done all that the Lord would have us do, we have accomplished all that matters.
4. We must learn to appreciate our pain and suffering, or we cannot fully appreciate the greatness of God's glory.
5. Jesus refused to give people a sign because *he* was the sign, which they didn't recognize.
6. The best encouragement comes from better recognition of God's miracles.
7. Perfection is a reachable goal when it suits God's purpose, but it's impossible, otherwise.
8. Children have God-given strength, believing they can reach up and touch the stars, as if God is only an arm's length away.
9. Having God's assurance of the truth is much more valuable than thinking we know the truth.
10. Without God's discernment, I have difficulty separating what is relevant from what is irrelevant.

Questions for Further Thought

- What makes one day more important than another?
- How might every day seem like a holiday?

Blind Society

In a blind society, nobody knows what it would be like to see.

Jesus didn't condemn blindness. He condemned the Pharisees who said they *could* see but didn't. We need to understand that God sees what we can't see, so we depend on him for guidance.

> *Right now, our knowledge and vision are limited, but the day will come when we will see as God does.*
> — *1 Corinthians 13:12*

Ten Thoughts to Ponder

1. When we fail to see God's hand at work, we call accidental good fortune "luck."
2. When tempted to do good, we feel good about ourselves. When tempted to do bad, we shouldn't look for someone else to blame.
3. Everyone on Earth is affected by positive and negative forces. Who we are and how closely we walk with the Lord determines whether our reaction will be positive or negative.
4. No amount of preparation can be a substitute for having God's help.
5. Vision is not a pathway to success unless it's God's vision.
6. One misunderstood Bible verse can be exceptionally destructive.
7. If we know God is our best resource for truth, we should wonder why anyone would choose to look elsewhere.
8. I'm not likely to find something lost if I don't know or don't care that it was lost.
9. If I knew where God was leading me and all that I am to do, I'd be tempted to say there wasn't any way.
10. Taking every thought captive is achieved by confronting one bad thought at a time.

Questions for Further Thought

- Why might we doubt that God saw what we never saw coming?
- What can we do when we see no way out of our troubles?

Healthy Diet

Jack bought six donuts and two apple fritters. Only the empty sack made it to the office. For lunch, he ate a triple-meat cheeseburger with fries and a strawberry shake. After every meal, he reminded himself how badly he needed to exercise and maintain a healthy diet.

His actions led to his heart attack, not what he told himself.

The Lord says, "Come now, let's correct the problem. ... When you desire what I want and do what I say, you will feast upon the good of the land."
— Isaiah 1:18–19

Ten Thoughts to Ponder

1. If we feel lost, we can be thankful that God knows where we are and will take us to where we need to be—if we're willing.
2. Temptation puts people in a situation where a choice must be made.
3. For my ears to be open to what God might say, I must get what I want out of the way.
4. When we don't want to know, the truth can't be seen.
5. Frustration is having a goal with no apparent means to get there.
6. As soon as I surrender my desires to him, God will carry the weight that's too heavy for me.
7. Rather than a statement of belief, salvation is best understood as total surrender to God's will.
8. The difference between Lord and lord is the degree of majesty, holiness, and power.
9. A treasure is very hard to find when you don't know what you're looking for.
10. Eternity is a very ... very ... very ... long time—longer than we can imagine.

Questions for Further Thought

- Why is it sometimes difficult to do what we say we should do?
- How can we change our desires so our actions match what we know is right?

Panic Attack

Who was the idiot who made up the FEAR acronym?—False Expectations Appearing Real. So were the panic attacks. Then she saw the truth that made the fear go away.

She had every reason to fear, because she had no control, but she had an even greater reason *not* to fear, since God was in control.

> *You are my salvation from all that would pull me down, so who is left for me to fear? My life is in your hands, so I have no reason to be afraid.*
> — *Psalm 27:1*

Ten Thoughts to Ponder
1. God's breakthroughs are greater than anything we can imagine.
2. Words without meaning are as palatable as sawdust.
3. We must surrender our selfishness before we can convey God's generosity.
4. Wanting what I want can be an obstacle to acquiring what I need.
5. Acting on impulse can be either good or bad, depending on whether God or something else is the driving force behind the action.
6. Vision has value—but only if it leads us to the next right step.
7. Trusting God requires surrender of what I think I need so I can accept his provision of what I *really* need.
8. Temptation is an invitation to do something, either good or bad.
9. I have no problem asking God for everything I want. That part is easy. The difficulty is accepting his answer.
10. If all I have for direction is my blindness, I am sure to wind up in the ditch.

Questions for Further Thought
- Why do people sometimes fear what they don't need to fear, yet have no fear of real threats that could kill them?
- When do people have a reason to fear what Satan might do?

Valiant in Battle

Out of twelve spies, only Joshua and Caleb believed God's promise that the Canaanite land would be theirs. Over the next forty years, all the unbelievers died, and the next generation conquered the land.

We can face life's challenges with confidence, but only if we know God is with us, giving us the strength and ability that we need.

Who can win the battle against the world? Only those who believe Jesus is God's Son.
— 1 John 5:5

Ten Thoughts to Ponder
1. Pursuit of the impossible dream is wasted time and effort unless it is what God wants.
2. God answers all prayers in the way he knows is best, not necessarily what we *think* is best.
3. Every feeling of God's presence is a potential breakthrough toward the fulfillment of his plan for our lives.
4. The obvious is seldom questioned, but it should be, if we want to be sure it is true.
5. What we can't see is invisible—until God opens our eyes.
6. God's miracles shout the truth of God's wisdom and power, but not for those who choose not to listen, because they want to hear something else.
7. Our failures are worthy of celebration when they are part of God's plan for our success.
8. Having my way may look like a treasure but it's actually worthless fool's gold.
9. God's plan is always worth whatever pain and suffering is needed for its fulfillment.
10. If God sees all things before they happen and *could* intervene, nothing can simply be coincidence.

Questions for Further Thought

- How can we know when something is worth fighting for or when we should surrender?
- What forces on Earth oppose what God wants to do?

Winning Odds

If Charlie won the lottery, he could have everything he wanted. All he had to show for his faith was losing tickets, because he had a better chance of being struck by lightning on a clear day.

From the Bible, he found the only sure way to win. He really could have everything he wanted. All he had to do was find a way to want only what God wanted. Then, as they worked together, even the impossible might be possible.

> *Delight in the Lord, for he can give you the desires of your heart when you want what he wants.*
> *— Psalm 37:4*

Ten Thoughts to Ponder

1. When the Lord is active in our thoughts and actions, our names have greater meaning and value.
2. Believing a lie requires less energy than embracing the truth.
3. Knowing *what* to do isn't enough. I still need God's help.
4. Tragedy is being too busy to find ways to save time.
5. Without the desire, doing what God wants is impossible, which is why we must pray for his will, not ours.
6. Since God requires only our effort, and he will take care of the results, excuses are unacceptable.
7. Accepting the truth can require a painful sacrifice of what we believe.
8. Asking lots of questions improves the probability of finding answers, because we give up our assumption that we already know.
9. Believing harder won't make anything more or less true.
10. Expecting artificial intelligence to replace human reasoning is not very intelligent.

Questions for Further Thought

- Why do people buy lottery tickets when they know they have virtually no chance of winning?
- Why might people be reluctant to want what God wants?

Last Breath

The freeway traffic was heavy, but the cars to my left and the flatbed truck in front of me were staying close to the posted 65 mph speed limit. The second exit ahead was mine.

I glanced up to see an irregularly shaped 2'x3' flat black object fly off the heavy equipment on the flatbed, sailing like a discus aimed at my windshield. I was only one breath away from seeing Jesus.

> *Keep watch, because you do not know the day or the hour.*
> *— Matthew 25:13*

Ten Thoughts to Ponder

1. Without a desire to spend the day profitably, I am likely to think I wasted a lot of valuable time.
2. Without the Lord guiding me, my talent for messing up is sure to show up.
3. Without the death of our desires, we won't see the resurrection of God's desires working naturally in our lives.
4. Faith looks for the city whose maker is God so we can live close to him forever.
5. The greatest of all servants has the greatest of all names.
6. My limited understanding of God gives me a vague image of who I am to become.
7. If Solomon had been as wise as his reputation claims, he would've said he only wanted whatever God wanted.
8. Nobody can *be* God, but we have his promise that we can be *like* him.
9. If I *want* to know, then I *will* know—provided God has a purpose in my knowing, and I have his assurance that what I think I know is actually true.
10. Humor can be disarming, allowing both subtle truths and also lies to slip in, unnoticed.

Questions for Further Thought

- Why should we believe we'll have many more days on Earth?
- What would you do if you knew the next month was to be your last days on Earth?

Pleasing the Big Boss

The big boss wasn't smiling. "If you can't do the job," he said, "I'll find someone who can."

Demand for performance permeates our society. That's why we might think we can't please the Lord. Not to worry. Because of his help, our effort will always be good enough.

> *We've prayed for your complete knowledge of God's will, with great wisdom and spiritual insight. May your lives honor the Lord as you work to please him in every way, increasing in knowledge.*
> — *Colossians 1:9–10*

Ten Thoughts to Ponder
1. In grieving, we struggle to accept the way things are so they can be made better.
2. We easily identify symptoms while the disease remains a mystery, often diagnosed incorrectly.
3. Telling people they're wrong isn't much help, because they already know that. What they need to know is why doing right is so much better.
4. HOPE is Having Our Patience Energized.
5. In trusting the Lord, I surrender my self-confidence.
6. When the gain is greater than the loss, we don't have to grieve.
7. God is the best of friends, because he knows everything about us, yet loves us more than we can imagine.
8. The more I know, the more I know that I don't know.
9. Unless the Lord helps us see the truth, we will never know what filthy rags we used to be, before he cleaned us up.
10. For the help I most need, I must look to the Lord when I don't know I need help.

Questions for Further Thought

- When we don't feel good enough to be successful, what can we do for assurance that we can please the Lord?
- In what ways can we trust God to use even our mistakes to accomplish his purpose in our lives?

Tired of Waiting

Samantha grew tired of waiting for the perfect opportunity. She needed to be doing something, so she decided to do her waiting as a waitress. After that, she wasn't tired anymore.

Exercise builds strength. Instead of waiting for God to do something, we can put on our work clothes to help someone now.

With better knowledge of the Lord, seek to master your desires,
learn to patiently wait upon him, and do what most pleases him.
— *2 Peter 1:6*

Ten Thoughts to Ponder

1. We can never do as much for God as he does for us, but we can do all he has for us to do.
2. To be clean within, we need more than soap and water. We need God's Word.
3. Unconditional surrender won't allow us to tell the Lord we can't do something he wants us to do.
4. Caring for everything God wants can free us from the cares of this world.
5. Those who want to go their own way will eventually get their way.
6. Without a sense of what the Lord would have me do, I will never know enough to make a competent decision.
7. Everything I learn about God is sure to change me in some way.
8. What God paid to save us from death makes our lives extremely valuable in fulfilling his purpose.
9. Speculation is a poor substitute for knowing the truth.
10. When our day is tragically different from what we hoped, the Lord is still our best hope for the day.

Questions for Further Thought

- Why do people wait for a better time when they could accomplish something right now?
- If books, seminars, and Internet searches contain all we need to know, why might experience still be the best teacher?

Pray a Lot

David said, "God sees me every time I sit up or sit down." Jesus said God sees every sparrow that dies, and we're worth a *lot* more than two sparrows.

God knows the number of hairs on my head, so he must know *everything* about me, better than I know myself, but I'm learning. This is why I pray a lot.

> *Pray continually, always mindful of God's presence.*
> — *1 Thessalonians 5:17*

Ten Thoughts to Ponder

1. Believing, we will tell God what we think he should do, but with *faith* we surrender to whatever he chooses to do.
2. We should praise God for the tests, temptations, and even tragedies when they bring us closer to God.
3. I need to do whatever God is waiting for me to do, but I still need his help.
4. For God to have his perfect way, I need to get out of his way.
5. I need the *reality* of God's presence much more than I need the *feeling* of God's presence.
6. God helping me with the little things will help me achieve whatever big thing needs to be done.
7. God's light from the Son is our energy source for life.
8. If I care for the right things, then I'm motivated to do the right things.
9. In the beginning, the sacrificed Lamb in the garden of Eden atoned for sin, but Jesus' resurrection and the work of the Holy Spirit was necessary to remove our sin nature.
10. If I care how much I care, I can exchange the cares of this world for what the Lord cares about.

Questions for Further Thought

- What kinds of prayers could fill every moment of the day without being redundant?
- At what point should we tire of praying and give up on ever receiving an answer?

Expiration Date

I noticed the expiration date on a can of tuna. I had to wonder what expiration date my life might have.

In the fifth grade, I read that the life expectancy for men was sixty-eight. After passing that age by a decade, I'm learning that I might not have an expiration date.

I am the resurrection and the life. Those who believe in me will live, even if they have died, and those who are living and believe in me will never die.
— *John 11:25-26*

Ten Thoughts to Ponder

1. Taking one step at a time as God directs will inevitably get us to where he wants us to be—if we are patient, never giving up.
2. God's light shining *upon* us is wonderful, but his light shining *through* us is even better.
3. God cannot fail, so if we think he has, we haven't understood the situation and his purpose.
4. If we really love God, we've forgiven our enemies because we love them so much.
5. We may not understand God's purpose, but we can be sure he has one, or we wouldn't be here.
6. "I'm not good enough" is a positive confession if we have faith in the Lord, who *is* good enough.
7. To see the fulfillment of God's promise, I need power to start, persistence to keep going, and patience.
8. If we knew God's plan for those who love him, words could not express our excitement.
9. Even God can't help people who don't want help.
10. We can believe anything, true or false, but to have faith in God, we must first hear his voice.

Questions for Further Thought

- Why do some people have little respect for life?
- If Heaven is so much better, why are people left on Earth?

Can't Buy Me Love

One of the great driving forces in life is to be loved and appreciated. The kind of love we're looking for is priceless. It can't be bought.

A better term for "lover" is "giver," an expression that is most evident when its focus is to help the utterly undeserving.

> *The immense greatness of God's love is proven by the fact that we were undeserving sinners when Christ died for us.*
> — *Romans 5:8*

Ten Thoughts to Ponder

1. A lack of time will limit what we can do, but God has all the time he needs to accomplish his purpose.
2. We most need to pray when we see no need to pray.
3. God's forgiveness alone won't get us into Heaven, but a born-again, changed life will.
4. An apology kisses the wound so hurting people will feel better.
5. Given the many questions I ask the Lord, I should probably ask what answers he would like to hear from me.
6. If we understand how insignificant we are, compared to God's majesty, we are already smarter than Satan was, when he fell from glory.
7. If we want to do better, we must present that desire to the Lord, for we can't make that happen without his help.
8. Dreams for a wonderful future are self-defeating if I can't do what I need to do today.
9. Apologies are empty words if we don't feel the other person's pain.
10. Our limited capacity to understand God is still enough to know that his value justifies our sacrifice of everything—if we want to know.

Questions for Further Thought

- What best indicates that expressions of love are genuine?
- Why might the recipient of a loving gift have no appreciation for its value?

Profitable Pursuit

Supposedly, success comes from planning our work and working our plans. However, neither Jonah nor Balaam did well with their plans. Maybe we need to rethink the importance of our pursuits.

We should know that God is smarter than we are, and he wants the best for us. Therefore, we'd be cheating ourselves if we got what we wanted when God wanted something else.

> *The past needs to be forgotten so I can ... focus entirely on the heavenly reward that comes in following Jesus Christ.*
> — *Philippians 3:13–14*

Ten Thoughts to Ponder

1. Becoming more like Jesus is worth the effort, no matter how long it takes.
2. When we say we have no choice, we're actually saying we've already made up our minds.
3. To go my own way, I must ignore God's presence.
4. Our burdens are much too heavy for us to carry alone.
5. I cannot leave for others what the Lord would have me do myself.
6. Without the death and burial of our desires, we won't see the resurrection of God's desires working naturally in our lives.
7. Surrender to the Lord requires recognition of what we will gain and what needs to be sacrificed.
8. My most desperate desire needs to be for whatever God knows I most desperately need.
9. If God is for us, giving up on him is the only way we can lose.
10. In the absence of love, when we don't care at all for others, we miss the opportunity for empathy and getting to say we're sorry.

Questions for Further Thought

- If our plans are so great, why do more than ten thousand U.S. businesses file for bankruptcy each year?
- Why might following the Lord seem to be wrong when it is actually right?

Godly Initiative

After bravely opening the business meeting with prayer, Jack glanced around the room, concerned for what the atheists might be thinking. "If you were offended by asking God for help," he said, "I'm sorry. But if there is no God, what difference does it make?"

With a godly initiative, we have everything to gain and nothing to lose.

People must hear the Word of God before they can believe it. Sin is failure to do the good you know you should do.
— *Romans 10:17; James 4:17*

Ten Thoughts to Ponder
1. With God's timing, I can know when to start or stop, walk or run, talk or listen.
2. Ignorance is not knowing. Foolishness is knowing but not doing.
3. Wishes are spinning tires with no movement forward.
4. Without tests and trials, we can't be sure whether our faith is real or imaginary.
5. I must let go of old habits before new practices can be applied.
6. We cannot describe an indescribable God, but we can benefit from trying.
7. Solving a problem at its root will take care of both the symptoms and the cause.
8. God is a phenomenal GPS, because he can guide me when I don't even know where I am going.
9. In the model prayer, we learn what our desire should be: to see God's will done on Earth as it is in Heaven.
10. Pleasing the Lord is the best way to satisfy our hunger.

Questions for Further Thought

- What is the difference between running *ahead* of God, *behind* God, and *with* God?
- Why might Christians be reluctant to take initiative when they already know what they should do?

Happy Birthday

When Jesus was born, only a handful of people knew how significant his life would be. Now, Jesus has the greatest of all names.

A life's value is recognized at the end, not the beginning. After we have fought well to fulfill God's purpose, our pleasing the Lord and helping others gives us reason to celebrate.

> *I have fought long and hard to finish this race, and I have not wavered, remaining faithful. A crown of righteousness awaits me.*
> — *2 Timothy 4:7–8*

Ten Thoughts to Ponder
1. Since our desires will control our choices either to obey or disobey, we need God's help in having the right desires.
2. Vision doesn't mean much if it is limited to what we see with our eyes.
3. I still have a lot to learn, and some of what I think I know needs to be unlearned.
4. Sharing your story is an opportunity to relive the experience, increase its value, and encourage others as well as yourself.
5. The necessity for pleasing God is understood by obedience, not by asking why.
6. Mindless choices are wonderful, but only if they come from having the mind of Christ.
7. If my interests conflict with God's desire, then who I am needs to change.
8. Pleasing the Lord should be our greatest delight.
9. There is method to God's madness that makes perfect sense to him, but not to me.
10. To hear the Lord, I must pay attention and avoid distractions.

Questions for Further Thought

- For what reasons might being born to wealthy and powerful celebrity parents be a disadvantage, not an advantage?
- What are the most important factors that lead children to grow in wisdom and favor with God and people?

Miracle Might

God didn't call Moses because he was a charismatic speaker. Gideon must have been shocked when the angel said, "Behold, mighty man of valor." When David was anointed by the prophet Samuel, nobody could have imagined him killing Goliath. They were miracle workers, not because of their talent, but because they were obedient.

If we're willing to accept his call, God will reward our effort and be responsible for whatever miracle he chooses to do.

God uses what the world regards as foolishness to embarrass those who think they are so smart. Through our weaknesses, he will do mighty things that confound those who hold positions of power.
— 1 Corinthians 1:27

Ten Thoughts to Ponder

1. If we're not comfortable with the truth, we should ask what lie has made us comfortable.
2. Understanding the truth is as important as hearing it.
3. Absolute certainty comes only by hearing and believing what God says is true.
4. Using what we *can* see, we interpret what we *can't* see but believe has to be there.
5. To sell a Gospel Truth, we must appeal to our prospect's great need.
6. Without God's direction, we can see what we *think* is urgent, yet miss what is most important.
7. Faith hears God's voice and believes when there is no proof.
8. With God's will, there's always a way—if we're willing.
9. When we follow the direction of the Holy Spirit, we can be prepared for what we don't know is coming.
10. Vision has negative value unless it changes our actions to do and say whatever God wants.

Questions for Further Thought

- Why might it be difficult to believe that all things are possible?
- What keeps talented people from always being successful?

Christmas Wishes

If I was a good little boy, I could expect hand-me-down clothes, a used toy, and maybe a new pair of jeans. My gifts depended on what my parents could afford.

Given his unlimited resources, I now know God will give me whatever I need, which is better than getting my wishes.

If you who are evil know how to give good gifts to your children, you can be sure your heavenly Father will give the Holy Spirit to those who ask him.
— Luke 11:13

Ten Thoughts to Ponder

1. Being used of God is a matter of surrender, not time, might, or money.
2. Of all the good things we might do, only one thing is most pleasing to the Lord.
3. People choose darkness to avoid the pain of being seen.
4. Satan loves taking the blame for our bad choices, because then we don't see the real reason.
5. My unconditional delight in the Lord allows him to give me the desires he wants me to have, and then get what I want.
6. Our choice for Heaven instead of Hell depends on wanting an eternity with the Lord above everything else.
7. Yesterday has negative value unless its lessons can improve what I do today.
8. For as long as I deny that conditions are what they are, they are not likely to improve from the way they are.
9. Open and honest questions encourage me to accept answers that I didn't anticipate.
10. Solutions have no value unless they help solve the problem.

Questions for Further Thought

- Why might parents be foolish in giving their children what they want instead of what they need?
- More than anything else, what thing of eternal value should we most want from God?

Driving Force

In my pedal car, I went wherever my little legs would take me. I imagined flying down the highway, but actually my desire to have fun took me down bumpy dirt paths and uneven, cracked sidewalks in the neighborhood.

Today, life's bumps can't be avoided, but driving wherever the Lord leads is an indescribable thrill.

> *Keep your physical desires under control and maintain your integrity and honor, not driven by fleshly desires.*
> *— 1 Thessalonians 4:4*

Ten Thoughts to Ponder

1. Depending upon our choices, our ability to believe whatever we want to believe will either be a curse or a blessing.
2. If we knew the right questions to ask, we'd have a better chance of discovering the right answers.
3. Whether God is *with* us or *after* us depends on whether we want to go *his* way or *our* way.
4. If we want to be concerned with what matters, we need to set aside our concern for what doesn't matter.
5. Living in God's presence, we can have access to whatever we need to know, whenever we need to know it.
6. I need to clear out all the rubbish before I can see the hidden filth that needs to be cleaned up.
7. Our goal is idolatry when it conflicts with what God wants.
8. Apart from a God connection, the human mind cannot distinguish reality from what it *thinks* is reality.
9. I wanted to be in control of my life until I discovered the greater value of respecting God's control.
10. By questioning my perception of reality, I hope to understand the reality that I don't understand.

Questions for Further Thought

- Why do some Christians believe their lives should go smoothly, without bumps and unexpected turns?
- How do we benefit from surviving tough times?

Dream Chaser

With all the practice and intense believing I can muster, my childhood dream of dunking a basketball can happen only if the goal is lowered by two feet.

Chasing after my dreams may not give me what I want, but following the Lord to get what he wants *can be* a slam dunk.

> *I focus entirely on the heavenly reward that comes in following Jesus Christ.*
> — *Philippians 3:14*

Ten Thoughts to Ponder

1. As we acquire more of God's nature, we can enjoy the success of others more than our own.
2. No sane argument has enough power to change the insanity that some people choose to believe.
3. If we love God, we have no choice but to share our stories how he has changed our lives, giving us peace, love, and forgiveness that the world cannot understand.
4. I long to have the right words to say, but I have a much greater desire to have the actions that matter more.
5. Scientists can search forever for the source of life, but they will never find it—unless they recognize God's presence.
6. Pain and suffering can be an essential factor in seeing our need for the Lord.
7. Imagination can see what isn't there but is not always able to detect what isn't real.
8. Thinking others know what we know can be a tragic mistake.
9. Without evidence, we cannot be convinced that the impossible is possible—unless we choose to believe.
10. For me to be the person God wants me to be, I must admit who I am, desire to change, and look to him for help.

Questions for Further Thought

- What reasons do people have for wanting anything other than what God wants?
- How can treasures on Earth have any eternal value?

Imaginary Friend

When I was young, I liked talking to my invisible friend. He was my faithful companion—always eager to hear what I had to say.

In God, I found an even better friend who went with me everywhere. When I imagine and talk to him, I'm communicating with someone who is as real as the people I can see.

No person has ever seen God face-to-face. But if we love others, we have him living within us and his love finds its full expression through us.
— 1 John 4:12

Ten Thoughts to Ponder

1. Given the fact that reality is from all the conditions that make it so, saying conditions shouldn't be the way they are is an argument against reality.
2. People who don't recognize God's presence will act as if he is nowhere around, unable to see the evil.
3. Those who have no respect for God's voice may sometimes listen to what he is saying through the actions of a friend.
4. The first step toward receiving God's help is to recognize his presence to know our thoughts and hear our prayers.
5. We do well to learn from our mistakes, but we have less pain in learning from the mistakes of others.
6. I wouldn't have to ask so many questions if I could remember what I already know.
7. Hope is what we must have to keep from giving up.
8. If I do my very best, I still need God's help to make my effort good enough.
9. Surrender to the Lord will turn failure into success.
10. With no respect for God's presence, people can imagine that either God doesn't exist or he is nowhere around.

Questions for Further Thought

- Why might people value the words of a psychologist more than the Word of the Lord?
- How can we prepare for the potential consequence of being open and honest?

Crying Good Time

In 1949, I used a key to turn the side screw and clamp each skate with four steel rollers onto the soles of my laced-up walking shoes. In those days, we didn't know about helmets and knee pads.

When I fell and skinned my knee, Mom kissed the wound to make the pain go away, and I was ready to skate some more.

Since my emotional wounds bleed and hurt worse than my physical cuts and scrapes, it's so good to know the Lord.

> *Since you know how much God cares, you can surrender all your worries to him.*
> — *1 Peter 5:7*

Ten Thoughts to Ponder

1. When one truth is added to another truth, we have an epiphany.
2. Since God knows all the conditions of our existence, his perception of reality is much better than ours.
3. The more respect I have for the Lord, the more I want to be with him and become like him.
4. When we become one of Jesus' disciples, we are eager to hear whatever he has to say.
5. The first lesson in learning is learning to listen.
6. What we think we know can be incorrect assumptions that lead to wrong conclusions.
7. The Holy Spirit, sent to guide us into all truth, will either confirm or dispute our beliefs—if we listen well.
8. While quietly sitting to understand the reality of my world, I desperately need God's help to see the reality I cannot see.
9. Separating fact from fiction isn't always easy, and that's a fact.
10. Our pain and suffering prove the reality of our faith and the value of the rewards ahead.

Questions for Further Thought

- Why might the words from a friend be more helpful than advice from a psychiatrist?
- What are the dangers of *stuffing* our thoughts and feelings?

Greatness of God

In October 1957, I stared into the night sky to see Sputnik I orbiting the earth. I built a telescope to get a better look at the moon, Jupiter, and Saturn, and I wondered what it would be like to see Earth from out there. At the time, nobody knew.

I find that the more I walk with God, the better I know him and appreciate his presence.

> *O Lord, creator of all things, you are worthy of all honor, power, and glory, because everything that exists was created for your good purpose.*
> — *Revelation 4:11*

Ten Thoughts to Ponder

1. To be Superman and do what I was called to do, I must have God's strength and avoid the kryptonite.
2. By focusing on needs for today, not tomorrow, I can make today much better. And tomorrow will be better, as well.
3. If I must do something independent from what God wants, then it's my great delight to have failed quickly so I can be about my Master's business.
4. When God's purpose becomes our purpose, then the work we do together cannot fail.
5. As soon as I sense that God could be working in my life, I am impressed as one seeing a miracle.
6. Before I do anything, I need to pray, just in case God has something to say.
7. Short is sweet when God is in it, but long can be lovely for the same reason.
8. Before I can expect God to help me, I expect that I must be about helping others.
9. If my life is about money, I'm a loud noise in an empty house.
10. Since God has made my work easier, I can work much harder.

Questions for Further Thought

- What can we do to comprehend an incomprehensible God?
- What are the most significant differences between God and Satan?

Personal Promises

As the glass slippers fit Cinderella but not her wicked stepsisters, God's wonderful promises are made for *all* who belong to him. When the shoe fits, you can make his promises personal by including your name.

> *For God so loved [Your Name] that he gave his only Son, so that everyone who believes in him will not die but will live forever.*
> — John 3:16

Ten Thoughts to Ponder

1. To hear God's voice, we must listen to what he's saying, not what we *want* him to say.
2. After so many years of thinking I needed to be in control, putting God in control of my life is a significant challenge.
3. People sometimes ask, "What would Jesus do?" But it's much more important for us to do what Jesus did.
4. The drudgery of work can become my great delight when I sense the Lord working with me.
5. The fact that I'm doing okay is not okay, because God's okay is so much better than my okay.
6. Pursuit of my own self-serving goals is not likely to work well for me, because I won't have God's help.
7. If we are paying attention, God will give us answers when we don't know we need one.
8. For all eternity, the awesomeness of God's presence will amaze me, because he will always be more than I can imagine.
9. Anticipation and preparation are important preludes to starting something new.
10. Impossible tasks include everything I so skillfully avoided by finding something else to do.

Questions for Further Thought

- How can we be sure that a promise God made to people in the Bible should apply to us?
- Under what conditions do we benefit from God's promises, and when might those promises be a curse?

Homework Help

When my son wanted homework help, he'd have been delighted for me to work the problems for him. When I had him read the textbook chapter again, he found that he didn't need my help.

Now I'm wondering how many times I'm looking to God for help when I'd do well to read his textbook again.

All scripture is inspired by God, important for teaching, correction, and discipline—for showing people how to live in righteousness.
— *2 Timothy 3:16*

Ten Thoughts to Ponder

1. In the midst of our afflictions, we have an opportunity to walk with the Lord and experience his miracles.
2. If I can convince myself that I am incapable, then I don't have to do anything.
3. If I want to be productive, I need to invest in God's plan, not mine.
4. A lot more things would be possible if I would quit procrastinating and just do them.
5. Self-determination and personal conviction can be significant obstacles when those desires conflict with hearing what God would say.
6. If we could see Heaven in all its glory, we would be more desperate to have our friends and family there with us.
7. In my dreams, I easily accomplish everything I imagine, but when awake, I do well to forget the dreams and get to work.
8. Those who forsake the Lord are proof that their loving Creator can't always have his way.
9. After working really hard to finish a project, laziness feels good—but not for long.
10. We steal what belongs to God by using his gifts for ourselves, not for *his* purpose.

Questions for Further Thought

- With conflicting views, how can we know who is right?
- What is so liberating about knowing the truth that hurts?

Reluctant Dishwasher

One day, I was the "dishwasher," meaning I had to wash and dry by hand all the dishes dirtied by a family of eight. I was watching TV instead, hoping Mom would take pity on me and do them.

"Frankie," Mom said, "you can choose to *like* or *hate* doing the dishes. But either way, you *are* doing the dishes."

I have glorified you on Earth by completing the work you gave me to do.
— *John 17:5*

Ten Thoughts to Ponder
1. That we were made for God's pleasure says we must be an expression of God's love to others.
2. If I'm not careful, I will listen to my own self-talk more than I listen to anybody else.
3. With total commitment to please the Lord, we enter the fiery furnace, experience God's presence as never before, and leave with praise beyond what English words can describe.
4. I must pray without ceasing because I'm not sure what God wants me to do, let alone how to do it.
5. Compared to the observation or sensing of God's presence, the *experience* of God's presence is much more delightful.
6. I can find plenty of promises in the Bible, but what I most need is to hear God's voice.
7. If I can't do what the Lord wants me to do today, then I have wasted the day.
8. Where our heart is—that's what determines what we choose to treasure most.
9. My imagination is real but thinking I can control God is not.
10. With complete confidence in God, knowing he is in control, I can accept my plight more easily.

Questions for Further Thought

- How can we learn to like the work that we would normally do our best to avoid?
- Why do some people not want to do what God wants?

Reluctant Giver

My three-year-old son was sitting in front of the TV, watching cartoons while eating his grapes from a bowl. Not once did he glance toward me sitting next to him.

"Don't you think it would be nice," I said, "to share your grapes with your dad?"

With a slight quiver in his lips, he handed one grape to me.

> *The measure you give determines the measure you will receive.*
> *— Luke 6:38*

Ten Thoughts to Ponder

1. Pain-and-suffering makes little sense to me when I cannot see God's purpose in it.
2. God's interest in talking to people is a miracle, but the greater miracle is that we can listen.
3. God is my Creator, so the only way I can be who he wants me to be is to accept his miracle-working transforming power.
4. The first step to seeing better is to recognize my blindness, then to trust the Lord to show me the way.
5. Since people can't change reality, they try to change people's perceptions to believe a lie.
6. Because I can't figure it out on my own, I need the Lord to show me where I am so I can get to where he wants me to be.
7. The hand of God at work, which I don't see, could be even more spectacular than the miracles or unexplainable coincidences that I do see.
8. When I mess up, I have God's encouragement to do better.
9. Confidence in God depends upon hearing God's voice, believing his word, and knowing the truth.
10. With God, we can run through a wall and leap over a troop, experiencing a miracle greater than what Scripture promises.

Questions for Further Thought

- Why does God love cheerful givers?
- How can we know how much we should give and how much we should keep for ourselves?

Greatest Gifts

Jesus should be our very best friend. He understands and supports us as we recognize the presence of his Spirit and strive to do what is important to him. He is our life, no matter whether we walk dirt paths or streets of transparent gold.

I'm thankful for many things, including the struggles that make me strong, but I'm most thankful for God's gift of himself.

> *If you who are evil know how to give good gifts to your children, you can be sure your heavenly Father will give the Holy Spirit to those who ask him.*
> — *Luke 11:13*

Ten Thoughts to Ponder

1. Discovery is most difficult when my eyes are closed and all I see is what I already know.
2. We need to pray without ceasing, because without fuel, the fires of inspiration quickly die.
3. With the Lord's guidance, I am able to do more than I know how to do.
4. With a multitude of other things I could be doing, I need the Lord's priorities for what I should be doing.
5. Satan would like to "bless" us with lots of stuff if our riches could separate us from God.
6. Spiritual exercise is a matter of the heart, not mind or body.
7. *Talking* is useless if it doesn't positively affect what I am *doing*.
8. When we aren't led of God, we don't know what to ask. Therefore, we risk asking for the opposite of what he wants us to do.
9. For an adequate perception of reality, I must somehow recognize God's greatness and my smallness.
10. If I want to accomplish more, I can't be content with only knowing what I know. I need the Lord to guide me.

Questions for Further Thought

- What are the best gifts that parents can give their children?
- Why should we covet the best gifts?

Especially Blessed

Typically, blessed Christians are perceived as happily married, living in nice homes, and having great jobs. With health and wealth, they feel good about their futures—which follows the world's perception of success.

However, the most blessed are actually like Mother Teresa, who give their lives in the service of others.

You have seen how we should work to help those in need. Remember that Jesus said greater blessing is found in giving, not receiving.
— Acts 20:35

Ten Thoughts to Ponder

1. By thanking God for his blessings, I can overcome my complaints about what I don't have.
2. Spiritual exercise gives us strength to overcome the desires of the flesh.
3. If I know how much better God's perspective is, then I can disregard my perspective and trust him.
4. Independent thought and novel ideas can be fatal when they are self-serving. Satan knows that but would never admit it.
5. God's guidance will help me only if I am willing to listen and follow his direction.
6. The best prayers are more a matter of being and doing than they are of wanting, explaining, and begging.
7. Spiritual exercise strengthens our spiritual muscles to produce physical results that are most pleasing to God.
8. Climbing the mountain to enjoy more of God's presence is worth all the strain and pain.
9. Pleasing the Lord comes from knowing what is most important to God, not what my flesh hungers for.
10. Accidents and coincidences happen all the time—which are surprising to us but not to God.

Questions for Further Thought

- How much should we be concerned about blessing others?
- What might cause a blessing to actually be a curse?

Daring to Be Different

On my first day in the second grade, I had to carry a big black metal lunch box shaped like a barn so I could have hot soup and cold milk from thermoses. How embarrassing. All the other kids brought a paper sack with a sandwich, chips, and an apple.

The next day, I anticipated pointed fingers and smirks aimed at me. Surprise. Several other kids now had lunch boxes like mine.

> *People will respect you if all you say and do sets a good example, revealing your complete trust in God and unconditional love for people.*
> — *1 Timothy 4:12*

Ten Thoughts to Ponder

1. To understand God's greatness, people may need to understand what he needs.
2. If we love the Lord and are working to fulfill his purpose, the question is how things working for *good* can be made *better*.
3. Learning is almost impossible if we think we already know.
4. To focus on spiritual exercise, I avoid physical distractions.
5. For an important discovery, we God to show us where to look, and then to know what to do with what we find.
6. Prayers are like incantations when they are offered with the intention of controlling God.
7. Depending upon what I value, I will sacrifice either more or less of my time, effort, and resources.
8. Patience is doing all we can, not sitting back, doing nothing, waiting for God to do something.
9. Our transformation is inevitable if we are to stand in the Lord's presence.
10. Since where we are and what we need to do is most important, where we have been and what we have done doesn't matter very much.

Questions for Further Thought

- Why are some people embarrassed for the public to see them as Christians?
- What distinguishes Christians from non-Christians?

128

Lost Key

After dinner, I gave my son my only key to drive our custom van. I hadn't yet put the new key on my key ring.

Back home from the restaurant, from the other side of the driveway, he pitched the key back to me. It hit my hand, but where did it go? I searched everywhere, even combing through the grass. I finally gave up.

Getting ready for bed, I happened to reach into my pocket and couldn't believe what I had found. The lost key.

> *My son was dead and has returned alive. He was lost but now is found. So they began to celebrate.*
> *The Son of Man came to seek and to save the lost.*
> — *Luke 15:24; 19:10*

Ten Thoughts to Ponder

1. If only God is good, then he must be our source for all good advice.
2. Fate is lying to us if it says we have no choice.
3. Hypocrites would rather *look* different than *be* different.
4. Praying for what I want is not as good as praying for what God wants.
5. With total surrender to the direction of the Holy Spirit, sinning becomes impossible.
6. Without faith, God's promises are beyond reach.
7. God gave his best to us, and he wants us to give our best.
8. Allowed to burn, sin is a fire that will burn your house to the ground.
9. Humility allows us to enjoy God's gifts.
10. Sinlessness is a "wedding" garment that allows us to stand before the Lord.

Questions for Further Thought

- What possessions are so important to us that we would do everything possible to avoid their loss?
- What are you hanging on to that would be a benefit if they were lost?

Amazing Grace

On a late afternoon, I was on the freeway headed east toward Dallas. The sun behind the mist from an isolated shower created a rainbow–a 360-degree circle of iridescent bands of color.

Beautiful beyond words. I wished for a camera.

Suddenly the shower turned to a downpour of hail, blanketing the windshield with solid white. I couldn't see. If I kept going, I would crash into someone. If I stopped, someone would crash into me.

Seconds later, the sky was blue. And I was thankful to be alive.

If I must walk through a gauntlet, you will protect me. ... With your strong right hand, you deliver me.
— *Psalm 138:7*

Ten Thoughts to Ponder
1. I find it difficult having to admit that I know, when I have so proficiently refused to admit that I know.
2. If I identify myself as something, then I excuse myself from having to be who I need to be.
3. What can't be accomplished in a month can be done in a day with the Lord's help.
4. Patience would be easy if it didn't take so long.
5. Who we are is important, but who we become matters more.
6. Taking one step in the right direction is guaranteed to get us to the right place—if we keep taking the next right step and refuse to give up.
7. *Saying* it well means nothing if we cannot *do* it well.
8. At birth, our names give us our identity, but our actions reveal who we really are.
9. The problem with thinking is not knowing what to think.
10. Makeup and masks are important to those who want to hide who they really are.

Questions for Further Thought

- How can we distinguish coincidence from a creative act of God?
- What must we do to be sure we're destined for Heaven?

Overwhelming Needs

A typhoon hits the Philippines, leaving hundreds of thousands homeless, without food and water. A famine in Africa threatens twenty-three million with starvation.

What should I do about such tragedies? With my limited resources, my prayer might accomplish more than a small donation. I do best by following whatever the Holy Spirit speaks to my heart.

> *If you sell what you have and give to those in need, you will store up treasure for yourselves in Heaven, where it is safe from moths and rust and thieves.*
> — *Luke 12:33*

Ten Thoughts to Ponder
1. Thinking we can do something without God's help is dangerous. It might be fatal.
2. Prejudiced people strengthen their beliefs by refusing to believe they could ever be wrong.
3. I am who I think I am, who others think I am, and who I think that others think I am. But I need God's help to see who I really am.
4. We are never too old or too young but are always just right for doing what God wants.
5. My most supercalifragilisticexpialidocious knowledge is nothing compared to what God knows.
6. Greed is the worst of all motivations, the antithesis of love.
7. Doing what God wants wouldn't be so hard if it were easy to give up what I want.
8. God seeks willing workers for the harvest, not a supervisor to tell others how the work needs to be done.
9. *Locomotive* is the crazy desire of the one-track mind.
10. Working because you love the Lord is better than working for his gifts.

Questions for Further Thought

- Why might money *not* be the answer to someone's needs?
- How can a loving God ignore people's needs?

Forewarned, Forearmed

Some people listen to psychics and consult horoscopes. Why? Feeling like we know the future gives us a sense of control. If the Lord isn't coming right away, we have time to play. Or do we?

On whatever day we draw our last breath on Earth, we face judgment and eternity. We need to be ready.

> *You do not know when the Son of Man will arrive.*
> — *Matthew 24:44*

Ten Thoughts to Ponder
1. To feel different about the way things are, we must change—and then the *situation* might change as well.
2. Knowing how *small* I am and how *big* God is, I can be fully dependent upon him and not think too highly of myself.
3. Feelings of resentment tell us lies, saying conditions should not be what they are, when they are what they are for all the reasons that they are.
4. Outside its ideal setting, the beauty of a diamond is missed.
5. Accepting the Lord requires accepting all that comes with the gift.
6. Without the challenges that God either causes or allows, putting the outcome of the day's events in doubt, our lives would be without adventure and boring.
7. The present is my great concern, because I can't do anything about the past and the future hasn't arrived.
8. God is the answer to all the questions I don't know to ask, because I am so busy asking questions I don't need to ask.
9. Learning from our mistakes keeps the cost from being a total loss.
10. A life-changing insight is an unexplainable breakthrough for the closed mind.

Questions for Further Thought

- How can we be ready when we don't know what is coming?
- Why do some who profess to be Christian think they'll be in Heaven as long as they do more good than they do bad?

Searching for Peace

I'm looking for peace in the midst of my storms.

If I expect peace in the *world*, I'm probably looking in the wrong place. Like the disciples in the raging storm on the Sea of Galilee, I see winds of terror and threatening waves. But if I know Jesus is with me in the boat, the world may be in turmoil, but I can be at peace.

> *I have told you these things so you will have peace because of me. In this world, you will suffer, but cheer up. I have overcome the world.*
> — *John 16:33*

Ten Thoughts to Ponder

1. After accepting the spark, we must deal with the heat from the resulting flames and anticipate a consuming fire.
2. Loving God's Word is more than a daily devotional Bible reading. It's listening for his voice.
3. All things are either caused or allowed by God.
4. I can be delighted with whatever happens if I have his assurance that he is in control.
5. I thought I was wrong until I found out I was mistaken.
6. I'm told that the price of burial sites is going up because of the cost-of-living increases.
7. I can't sacrifice my desires and accept what God wants—unless I trust him completely.
8. We shouldn't worry about a possible error in Scripture. God chiseled his Ten Commandments in stone, and people didn't respect those words either.
9. Total agreement is needed for boring, unproductive meetings.
10. With acceptance of a lie, which is *our* truth, it is next to impossible to accept the true truth—but with God, all things are possible.

Questions for Further Thought

- If Jesus is the answer to the internal peace that so many people are searching for, why is his peace so hard to find?
- What is the difference between the peace that the world has to offer and what's available through Jesus Christ?

Growing Up

"Frankie," Grampa said, "what do you want to be when you grow up?"

I said, "A farmer." He was a farmer. I wanted to be like him.

Some of my school teachers wanted me to pursue their interests—math, science, or music. Nobody suggested I should be a writer or speaker. Obviously, I had no talent there.

If God were to say, "Frankie, what do you want to be when you grow up?" I would answer, "I just want to be like you."

Fully commit your life to whatever God has called you to do.
Always be humble and gentle, allowing others to be different from you,
even in their faults, because you love them.
— Ephesians 4:1–2

Ten Thoughts to Ponder

1. When prisoners escape, they don't intend to change, but the Lord's release from prison comes with transformation.
2. If God loves a cheerful giver, he would certainly appreciate my eager acceptance of whatever he wants me to do.
3. To accept God's will, I must abandon my independent, self-serving desires.
4. I'm too blind and slow to dodge a bullet without God's guidance.
5. Listening well is impossible for people who don't know and understand their audience.
6. Without inspiration from the Lord, I don't know whether to cultivate and water my ideas or let them die.
7. Having an unanswered question is much better than drawing a wrong conclusion.
8. When I think I can do it, I'm in danger of thinking I don't need God's help.
9. Without trust, people don't listen.
10. Purpose is bad trouble when it's not from the Lord.

Questions for Further Thought

- Why do some adults in their forties act like children?
- What are the most important signs of maturity?

134

Sleeping Well

Some people lie if they think they'll benefit. They'll steal if they think they won't be caught. In a way, that's true for me.

If I told a lie or stole a penny, I would know. And God would know too. That's an overwhelming majority in my court. I don't want to live with a liar and a thief. I know I can't benefit from lying, and I'd sure be caught if I stole anything.

Being always honest and truthful, I can sleep well.

As God changes us and we no longer condemn ourselves, then we have greater confidence in him.
— *1 John 3:21*

Ten Thoughts to Ponder

1. If I anticipate none, I am impressed when I have one, and more can be overwhelming.
2. In God, we should be thankful for our losses as well as our gains.
3. God's "no" is a redirection, not a rejection.
4. The ability to slay giants doesn't have to be a concern—if we are walking hand-in-hand with the Lord.
5. Satan loves Scripture because he can make it say whatever he wants.
6. Life's greatest delights come when we and God can take pleasure in the same things.
7. One of God's great thrills is seeing all things work together for good when we couldn't believe they possibly could.
8. The sinner who doesn't fear death has no reason to repent.
9. If we know God is with us and always will be, we can be content with what we have.
10. God doesn't change, for he has no flaws and never makes a mistake. But he is one who does things that have never been done before.

Questions for Further Thought

- What aspect of sin gives people pleasure?
- How can we have a completely clear conscience?

Simple Prayer

When our nation was founded, selections from the King James Bible provided texts for students learning to read. Recognizing God, understanding sin, and reciting prayers were part of public education.

When I was two, I couldn't yet read, but I recited the prayer on the plaque above my bed. *Now I lay me down to sleep, I pray thee, Lord, my soul to keep. If I should die before I wake, I pray thee, Lord, my soul to take.* In this simple prayer, I daily acknowledged God's presence and found comfort in his protection.

> *Go to your room, close the door, and pray to your Father without being seen. Then your Father will see what you have done in secret and will reward you.*
> — *Matthew 6:6*

Ten Thoughts to Ponder
1. Work on Earth prepares people for Heaven or Hell.
2. My most desperate need for God's help comes when I don't think I need his help.
3. God's gift of free will says we will never get away with blaming others for our bad choices.
4. Wisdom chooses the right tool to handle the nuts.
5. Without the Lord to guide my thoughts, I don't know what to say and do.
6. Impatience will miss the gifts that are worth waiting for.
7. God never goes too far, and he never comes up short, because everything he does is exactly right.
8. Fear has torment, but love offers an adventure.
9. To satisfy our ignorance, we credit analysts for their speculation and pay consultants for their perceptions, assuming they know the truth that only God can know.
10. The darkness I have had in my life makes me highly qualified to radiate the brilliance of God's glory.

Questions for Further Thought

- Why do people pray for what they want, not what God wants?
- When might *doing* be more important than *praying*?

Life-or-Death Choice

In the Garden of Eden, God left the forbidden Tree of Knowledge accessible and then allowed Satan to tempt Eve, giving her a desire to eat the fruit when otherwise, she wouldn't have had a reason.

What was God's plan? He would reveal the extent of his love.

People could recognize their need for him. repent of their wrongdoing, and choose to love him more than their own way.

> *You cannot be the slave of two masters. You will either hate the one and love the other, or be devoted to the one and despise the other. You cannot serve both God and earthly treasure.*
> — *Matthew 6:24*

Ten Thoughts to Ponder

1. If I can discover a useful lesson from the trivial, the information is no longer trivial.
2. Worry about the problem is avoided only when we can see the solution that comes from God's hand at work.
3. I can't measure the value of time spent if I don't know what the Lord wants the time used for.
4. Anger adds fuel to an already destructive fire.
5. Not knowing where to look, I will search for answers in all the wrong places.
6. *Persistence* is your choice, but *insistence* depends on the choice of others.
7. The creative mind can see what *isn't* there.
8. Just one word from the Lord is worth more than ten thousand independent thoughts.
9. With prayer, we mail our letters to God with the right postage.
10. I was unqualified until God saw my weakness and knew his miracle-working power qualified me to do what he wanted.

Questions for Further Thought

- Why does pleasing God look like a good choice to some people but not to others?
- What might keep people from learning the lessons that would save them from death and lead to eternal life?

Special Delivery

The priest Zechariah couldn't believe God's miracle, not even when the message came through an angel. If I think I would have reacted differently, I need to consider his situation. His wife was much too old to have *any* chance of having a baby. No doubt, he had sought the Lord for years, in prayer believing he would give him a son. It hadn't happened. Now, there was no *reason* to pray.

Without hope, I may question whether my prayer will give me what I want. But when I've surrendered my will to him, I have *every* reason to have faith, believing God will have his way.

With your great power and mighty outstretched arm, Lord, you made the universe and the earth where we live. Nothing is too difficult for you.
— *Jeremiah 32:17*

Ten Thoughts to Ponder

1. With the great pleasure of God's presence, we can have joy, joy, and even more joy deep down within our hearts.
2. If God wanted to change the way things are, he could. And *when* he wants to, he will.
3. In the high winds, I can stand full of hope and confidence, knowing everything will be all right—if the Lord is with me.
4. Religious leaders fear the people, not the Lord, which is a bad mistake.
5. The Holy Spirit made it possible for Jesus to know whatever he needed to know, whenever he *needed* to know.
6. Those who love the Lord will always have the resources available for whatever he has for us to do.
7. Being lost without the Lord is the worst kind of "lost."
8. Jesus is the perfect example of a son who is like his father.
9. "Certainty" allows us to share the truth among people who don't agree.
10. Knowing God takes all the guesswork out of reality.

Questions for Further Thought

- Why might we think our way is more important than God's?
- How does our believing affect what God will do?

Roaring Writer

When I was a kid, I had laryngitis. My mother said that was a blessing. I called it *frustrating*. I had to write notes to say anything. With an infection in both ears, I felt like I was at the bottom of an empty well, barely able to hear what others were saying. That's as close as I can get to imagining the struggle a man would have if he were suddenly struck deaf and dumb like Zechariah in the Bible.

Now, since I am neither deaf nor dumb, I have a responsibility to share my stories that might bring people closer to the Lord.

> *The Lord says you are his witnesses, his servants summoned to testify so people will know he is their Creator, that he alone is God forever and there will be no one else.*
> — Isaiah 43:10

Ten Thoughts to Ponder

1. God is our only sane reason for boasting.
2. Compared to the cost of *doing*, the cost of *trying* can be ridiculously expensive.
3. In Heaven, I anticipate no special reward, because all I've been doing is what the Lord had for me to do.
4. When people lie, they must ignore the truth.
5. In that which is temporary, we have hope for something that will be much better—and permanent.
6. "If it pleases the King …" should be my constant concern.
7. Artificial intelligence has no ability to hear and understand God's voice.
8. No matter how many people are with me, if I fail to recognize *God's* presence, I can feel very much alone.
9. Rolling the dice is a gamble—unless God controls the roll.
10. God's *present* purpose and actions supersede what he has said and done in the past.

Questions for Further Thought

- Why might Christians be reluctant to share their testimonies?
- How can you best illustrate what God has done to change your life?

Message Appeal

A man convinced against his will is of the same opinion still. That truism has been stated in different ways for centuries.

On Mars Hill, the apostle Paul said to the citizens of Athens, "I have seen that you are exceptionally religious, giving great honor and respect to all gods." Instead of condemning their worship, he directed them to the unknown God who deserved their worship.

Be gracious with your stories, flavoring your message with that which will answer the hunger in everyone's heart.
— Colossians 4:6

Ten Thoughts to Ponder

1. I can be comfortable in not knowing as long as I know I don't need to know.
2. As a trumpet vine cannot produce grapes, the proud can't bear good fruit.
3. Those who recognize royalty and bow humbly before God will be lifted up.
4. The drunkard doesn't remember where he has been or know where he is, nor can he see where he is going.
5. Those who know God as their provider have no reason to think luck will give them more.
6. Before I *listen* to what God is saying, I must *hear* his voice.
7. Wise men will pray for God to take away their pain and suffering, and they will thank him when he says, "Later."
8. No day, hour, or moment can be wasted if we're following what the Lord would have us do.
9. I have no idea how I could come up with an idea until God gave me an idea.
10. I'm not capable of a life-giving idea on my own, without God's help.

Questions for Further Thought

- What makes a person's message credible?
- Why might someone not be willing to believe God's angel who was sent with a message?

No Argument

When I was a kid, I believed Jesus loved me because the Bible said so. If today's culture doesn't respect the authority of Scripture, the worst thing we can do is quote a verse that people wouldn't believe.

The best we can do is tell our stories in a way that the experience is undeniable evidence or point to the truth of what they do believe.

This God created our world and everything in it ... desiring that we search and find him, though he is not far from any one of us. In him we live and move and have our being, *as your own poet Epimenides has said, for we are his children.*
— *Acts 17:24–28*

Ten Thoughts to Ponder

1. Faith is spiritual knowing that reaches past believing harder.
2. The stronger my belief, the more committed I am to believe, even if I'm wrong. So I need God's help to be sure I'm right.
3. The proof of our salvation is whether we endure until the end.
4. If I am busy doing whatever the Lord would have me do today, I have no reason to worry about tomorrow.
5. The Holy Spirit can cause us to know what otherwise we could not possibly know.
6. Before we do so much speculation without a conclusive answer, we might see if the Lord has anything to say.
7. The sound of silence requires careful listening to appreciate what isn't there.
8. Most of what we see has to be temporary, because most of what is eternal exists in the spiritual realm that we cannot see.
9. If we want to hear God's voice, we should do our best to eliminate the interfering noise.
10. If our relationships on Earth are important to us, we should be even more concerned about our relationship with the Lord.

Questions for Further Thought

- Why might people argue in favor of a point when they know they're wrong?
- When is a dispute worth arguing? When should we be silent?

Practically Speaking

I wonder how often we have a *feeling* about God's words but if asked what a certain verse meant, we wouldn't know what to say.

In practicing God's presence, I can put God's presence into practice by personalizing Scripture, applying his Word to understand my walk with him. King James might turn over in his grave if he knew I was messing with his words, but making the words personal is what gives us life.

> *Be content with whatever God provides, for he has said he will never leave us. He will never forsake us as orphans.*
> — *Hebrews 13:5*

Ten Thoughts to Ponder

1. When we make a mistake, it's time to step back, ask the Lord what went wrong, and take the next step in the right direction.
2. God speaks in a whisper to see whether we really want to hear what he has to say.
3. God is our superhero because he makes a way through walls without doors.
4. After spending time and effort doing all I know to do, I still need to spend time and effort to pray.
5. The difference between impulsive Peter and impulsive Jesus was the force behind the impulse.
6. Religious people seek respect that belongs only to God.
7. With focus upon quality, a little is worth more than a lot.
8. We will keep regretting our badness—until we can erase those memories with God's goodness.
9. I don't do the things I used to do. I don't think the things I used to think. But I'm still not doing everything I could do.
10. To listen, I must value what I am hearing.

Questions for Further Thought

- What does it mean to be so heavenly minded that we are of no earthly good?
- How can we be more effective communicators when we sense that our audience doesn't understand what we're saying?

Nice to Be Needed

The preacher said, "It's not about you," suggesting a truism we should all accept without question. Supposedly, it's all about God, as if I need God, but he doesn't need me.

If he didn't need us, then he had no reason to create us. If my life depends on him, then my extreme need for him makes it all about me, not all about him. The truth is, life is all about the relationships, about our need for God and our need for one another.

The power of God is at work in you to accomplish his purpose and make you his great delight.
— *Philippians 2:13*

Ten Thoughts to Ponder
1. My greatest problem with ignorance is not knowing that I don't know.
2. Adam disobeyed God so he could be with Eve, and Jesus obeyed God, entirely without sin, so we could be with him.
3. My next important step is whatever God wants.
4. We should know the apostle Paul was right when he said we can't sin when the Holy Spirit is our guide.
5. When God chooses to do a new thing, the old thing becomes obsolete.
6. If all we can believe is what we were told when we were growing up, we will never grow up.
7. Children can easily hear and believe God, because they haven't learned all the reasons *not* to believe.
8. When people refuse to admit the evidence, they have no choice but to believe a lie.
9. When the rich treasure possessions more than God's presence, they can't enter the Kingdom of God.
10. Sin is like a prescription bottle describing the benefits without revealing the side-effects.

Questions for Further Thought

- What can we do to make ourselves valuable?
- Why might rich people feel like they aren't good enough?

Genuine or Artificial

In high school, I had two ways to ace a test. Either I made sure I had learned everything I could, or I memorized details just before the tests, then forgot it all afterward.

I wonder how many Christians want to *look* good rather than *be* good. Meditating upon God's Word can change us on the inside so we aren't just *appearing* to be righteous.

> *You are like whitewashed tombs that look great on the outside but are full of dead men's bones and rottenness. Meditate upon what the Lord would have you do, completely surrendering yourself to his will so others will benefit from your relationship with him.*
> — *Matthew 23:27; 1 Timothy 4;15*

Ten Thoughts to Ponder

1. If I could let go of wishing I could do what I can't do, I'd have more energy to do what I need to do.
2. I need God's wisdom to gain the right knowledge ... understanding ... and finally ... more of his wisdom.
3. Hearing can be fatal when we listen to the wrong voices.
4. Given my nature for independence, my dependence upon the Lord must be a conscious choice.
5. If I want the Lord to reward me with more, I should give serious thought to doing more for him.
6. Learning means nothing without further thought.
7. Trying to fulfill God's purpose without his help is a case of grand theft—stealing God's vision as if it belonged to me.
8. Without faith, great expectations will become great disappointments.
9. The Bible contains a wealth of wonderful truth if we can avoid the misunderstandings and religious prejudices.
10. Talking too much is the best way for me to expose my ignorance.

Questions for Further Thought

- Why might trusting artificial intelligence be dangerous?
- What makes counterfeit money valuable?

Tough Love

A few spankings helped me decide whether I wanted to be good or have my own way. What Daddy wanted was important, but what my heavenly Father wants now is a much greater concern. Daddy loved me very much, but God cares for me even more.

The more I value my relationship with the Lord, the more I can't bear the thought of ever disappointing him.

> *If you love me, you will do what I tell you to do. I will ask the Father, and he will give you another Guide, one who will always be with you.*
> — *John 14:15–16*

Ten Thoughts to Ponder

1. To receive God's promise, we must be patient, because we think we're ready, but God knows we're not.
2. Independence from the Lord is a death sentence. In dependence, we have life.
3. If conditions should be anything different from what they are, the conditions would have to be different.
4. Our most gratifying expressions of "I'm sorry" are for conditions that are not our fault.
5. Pain and punishment can be necessary incentives when my desires are taking me in the wrong direction.
6. If I'm going to practice God's presence, I need to put God's presence into practice.
7. Learning from my successes is much more fun than having to learn from my mistakes—but not learning at all is a tragedy.
8. We can't *earn* love. Our choice allows us only to *give* love.
9. Meditating upon God's Word can change us on the inside so we aren't just *appearing* to be righteous.
10. The *perception* of progress does little more than make us feel good about ourselves.

Questions for Further Thought

- How might God's love differ from typical love on Earth?
- Why doesn't God always give us what we want?

So Near but So Far

Every day, a man dragged himself to the Bethesda pool with the hope of being healed when an angel stirred the water. But there was a problem: he couldn't move fast enough. He was left to accept his plight, doing like others around the pool—until Jesus came.

I wonder how many people today are like that man, living an apparently hopelessness situation, unaware of how close the Lord is.

Move closer to God, and he will move closer to you. He is not far from any one of us.
— *James 4:8; Acts 17:27*

Ten Thoughts to Ponder

1. Too much dreaming about the future ruins the value of today.
2. With great confidence in what the Lord is doing, I can let go of my apprehensions and do whatever he would have me do.
3. Confidence is difficult to achieve when I know I don't know.
4. If I don't learn from past mistakes, the present will suffer as well as the future—until I finally learn what I need to know.
5. I struggle with asking for what I want, because I most want whatever God wants.
6. God is preparing us for a future we can't see—giving us experiences, knowledge, and ability we didn't know we needed.
7. One might expect opposite personalities to avoid each other, refusing close contact, but that's not the way magnetism works, where opposite poles attract.
8. If what's important to God is important for me, I need to adjust my priorities.
9. Accepting truth is difficult when it is not socially acceptable or is not what we want to believe.
10. If I want the prize, I must endure the pain to get there.

Questions for Further Thought

- If God knows our thoughts and sees our actions, why do people think he's far away?
- How do we move closer to God?

Plugged In

I flipped the switch on my vacuum cleaner. Nothing. Evidently, the switch was broken. I pushed the switch off and back on. Still nothing. Then I noticed the problem. The cord wasn't plugged in.

Reminder to self: when turning on my prayer switch, be sure you're plugged into the power source.

The Lord Almighty says neither by might nor by power, but by my Spirit. You will receive power when the Holy Spirit comes upon you.
— *Zechariah 4:6; Acts 1:8*

Ten Thoughts to Ponder

1. In doing what the Lord would have me do today, I'm already experiencing a portion of eternity with him.
2. I would like to know many things I don't know, but I must trust the Lord to teach me whatever it is that I need to know.
3. I need help to understand God's madness, because what he does is always perfect to fulfill his purpose.
4. In the beginning, God made man in his image, but with Jesus, God made *himself* man to make us one family.
5. Confidence gives me a good feeling that I know what I know, but that doesn't prove I really know.
6. Willpower is either good or bad, depending on whether it is focused upon doing God's will.
7. When out of touch with who God is and what he is doing, people live in a reality of their own making.
8. By recognizing my need for the Lord, I avoid some painful experiences necessary to teach me how much I need him.
9. Compared to what God knows, all the artificial intelligence that human genius can create adds up to nothing.
10. The most impossible dream is to be like someone else, but I *can* be like Jesus because I have his help.

Questions for Further Thought

- How can we know when the Holy Spirit is leading us and not our own desires?
- Why did Jesus withdraw from people for private prayer?

Seeing Better

Bobby looked everywhere, even on the tool bench in the garage.

His mom said, "If they were a snake, they would bite you."

The next Sunday before church, he pulled his Bible down from the shelf. Clink! There were his eyeglasses on the floor.

We should always want to see better. The snake won't help us.

> *I fear that Satan might somehow tempt you as he did Eve, twisting your minds to believe something other than the simple message of complete surrender to Christ.*
> — *2 Corinthians 11:3*

Ten Thoughts to Ponder

1. Like a hospital, church should welcome the sick, the servant, and the visitor—not be like a theater or restaurant just for entertainment or fine cuisine.
2. A message sent isn't always received, let alone understood.
3. If order didn't matter, SPOT, TOPS, POTS, OPTS, and STOP would mean the same thing.
4. Unapplied learning is a waste of time and energy.
5. If Jesus increased in wisdom and favor with God and man, his growth required learning from his Father what he didn't know—until he *needed* to know, and *then* he knew.
6. Even when we don't know what the Lord wants, we can safely say yes to him. Always.
7. Without a deep desire to know the way it really is, we leave ourselves vulnerable to accept the mere appearance of truth.
8. Thinking I have the answer, I fail to ask questions that would reveal the truth I need to know.
9. Satan unwillingly does everything God wants, or he wouldn't be allowed, by his own evil nature, to do what he does.
10. If I can have the Lord's help to accomplish what needs to be done today, I don't need to be concerned about the future.

Questions for Further Thought

- Why are the blind sometimes unaware that they can't see?
- What do we need so we can see better, spiritually?

Strange Kind of Love

The most shocking exhortation the Jews ever heard from Jesus may have been to "love your enemies." Justice called for an eye for an eye, a tooth for a tooth, not forgiveness.

As we love others, especially the undeserving and those who might harm us, we can be free from anger and resentment and experience the abundance of God's love.

> *If your enemy is hungry, prepare a feast for him. If he is thirsty, give him your best wine. Your generosity will amaze him—as much a shock as coals of fire being poured upon his head—and God will reward you.*
> — *Romans 12:20*

Ten Thoughts to Ponder

1. When I compare *before* and *after*, I am filled with praise for God's miracle-working power.
2. What I treasure needs to have eternal value, or I might be wasting my time.
3. What God wants to create in us now is much different from who we were in the beginning and who we are yet to become.
4. I can always talk to God, because he's as close to me as my heartbeat.
5. If Solomon had spent more days walking with the Lord, he never would have said there was nothing new under the sun.
6. Studying to support beliefs is not as good as seeking the truth.
7. If I want something, I obviously don't have it, but before I worry about how to get it, I need to know whether God wants me to have it.
8. When we think we understand, we may have reached a higher level of stupidity.
9. The biggest lie I can tell myself is: *Sometimes I do what I don't want to do.* All things considered, we *always* do what we want.
10. Endless preparation accomplishes nothing.

Questions for Further Thought

- Why might people think it's impossible to love an enemy?
- By what criteria should God's children have what they want?

Ways to Remember

Whenever Peter heard a rooster crow, he remembered denying the Lord, weeping bitterly, and then experiencing God's love, mercy, and forgiveness. When I glance at my watch, I see time is short. I'll soon see the Lord. In nature, I am awed by the wisdom and power of my Creator. In seeing a car accident, I think of times I might have died.

We should be thankful for ways to remember God's goodness.

I remember when you helped me through hard times and marvel at what you've done.
— Psalm 143:5

Ten Thoughts to Ponder

1. We should appreciate and enjoy our differences, because God made us this way.
2. With complete faith in God's control, we don't have to be disappointed with what appears to be so bad.
3. Saying, "It could've been worse," is poor recognition of God's plan, because we could've said, "It will get better."
4. Based on myths and fantasies that we call *evidence*, we are free to accept whatever we want to believe,
5. The power of prayer is in knowing what God wants and not asking for what we want.
6. Jesus is the Father's connection with humanity as much as he is humanity's connection with the Father.
7. A change for the good will turn out really bad if it's not what God wants.
8. What God wants to create in us now is much different from who we were in the beginning and who we are yet to become.
9. If I am to fulfill all that God has for me to do, I must have his help with the obstacles.
10. Adventure can be exciting if we know God is in control, but otherwise, we have reason to fear.

Questions for Further Thought

- Why do we sometimes need reminders of God's truth?
- What prevents our forgetting the things we want to forget?

About the Author

Frank Ball was born in Kansas and became a naturalized Texan after moving to the Gulf Coast in 1954. After high school graduation, his forty-dollars-a-week salary as an office supply deliveryman required careful management. Half went to help support his parents, three younger brothers, and two sisters. The rest paid his ten-dollar-per-month car payment, filled the gas tank for less than 20 cents per gallon, and left a little pocket change for fun. Success came the old-fashioned way. He earned it.

Computer programming and business administration paid the bills. But in 1992, he began to abandon that love to pursue excellence in what he had most hated—writing—so he could compile a story for people who had heard of Jesus but didn't know much about what he said and did.

For ten years, he directed North Texas Christian Writers to help members improve their writing and storytelling skills. In 2011, he founded Story Help Groups and joined the Roaring Writers ministry seven years later to encourage and equip all Christians to tell their life-changing stories. Besides writing his own books, Frank Ball does ghostwriting, copy editing, and graphic design to help others publish high-quality books. He coaches writers, writes blogs, and is a panelist on The Writer's View, an email discussion group.

He has taught at writer's conferences and churches across the U.S. and Canada. As Pastor of Biblical Research and Writing for three years, he wrote sermons, teaching materials, and hundreds of devotions.

His first book, *Eyewitness: The Life of Christ Told in One Story*, puts all the biblical information on the life of Christ into a chronological story that reads like a novel. *Born Blind: Voice of a Visionary* is a novel about the first-century blind Jew who was healed when he washed his eyes in the Siloam pool. *The Discussion Bible* has thousands of unanswered discussion questions to stir people's thoughts. *Storytelling at Its Best* is a practical guide for effective storytelling.

Career Years

Frank worked in the business world for forty years. Titles he has held are Salesman, Sales Manager, VP of Sales, Executive VP, Computer Programmer, Systems Analyst, VP of Information Systems, Purchasing Manager, Personnel Manager, and VP of Production. In all his years in business, he spent nights and weekends doing biblical research, teaching, preaching, and counseling. In 1996, he became a part-time writer seeking to tell the gospel story in a way that people who didn't read the Bible would know about Jesus. Ten years later, he became a full-time freelance writer, teacher, and speaker, encouraging people to discover their stories and learn to tell them well.

Growing Up:

Frank's birth certificate says he was born in 1945 in Manhattan, Kansas. At that time, a gallon of milk cost 62 cents, a loaf of bread was 19 cents, and gasoline was 16 cents per gallon. His family moved to the Houston area in 1954 and to Fort Worth in 1962. He was working part time at the age of twelve, and has held the following jobs. (1) Egg Salesman, (2) Janitor, (3) Elevator Operator, (4) Dish Washer, (5) Computer Programmer, (6) Warehouseman, (7) Welder, (8) Roofer, (9) Lawn Care Professional, (10) Leather Craftsman, (11) Personnel Manager, (12) Computer Hardware Technician, (13) **Auto Mechanic**, (14) Deliveryman, (15) Office Supply Salesman, (16) Freelance Writer, (17) Copy Editor, (18) Associate Pastor, (19) Public Speaker, (20) Business Consultant, (21) Counselor, and (22) Carpenter. One item in the list was work without pay.

Frank is a widower since 2003, when his wife of thirty-seven years died of primary pulmonary hypertension. He has three married sons and seven grandchildren. He lives in an upstairs apartment, built in the huge attic of his oldest son's house in a Fort Worth suburb.

More Books by the Author

Eyewitness: The Life of Christ Told in One Story

All the Bible's information about Jesus in a chronological story that reads like a novel. Better than a harmony of the Gospels where we lack information from non-Gospel biblical text and have to mentally merge details from different Gospel accounts.

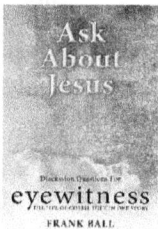

Ask About Jesus

A companion guide for use with *Eyewitness: The Life of Christ Told in One Story* for private meditation or group interactions. Thousands of thought provoking questions can stir our passion to know the Lord better and bring us closer to him.

Eyewitness Inspiration: Contemporary Vignettes for Life

A collection of stories based on faith, fantasy, and facts that reveal the motives of historical figures as well as the passion of people as ordinary as your next door neighbors.

God's Plan

A six-week chronological study of the life of Christ covering the period from the beginning to Jesus at age twelve. In each session's stories, the storytelling style retains the biblical and historical information, yet gives you the kind of captivating experience you'd find in a bestselling novel.

The Discussion Bible

All sixty-six books of the Bible in easy-to-read verses. Thousands of questions encourage personal insight, open for people to freely speak their minds without fear of being wrong.

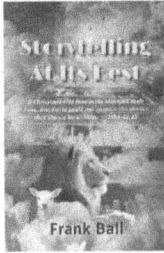

Storytelling at Its Best: A Practical Guide to Effective Storytelling

Storytelling at Its Best goes beyond common writing practices to focus on what will make your stories captivating. Learn the simple SCOOP IT UP with its seven essential storytelling blocks to find your best storyline. Practice building great sentences with sharp detail and vivid color, with dialog and action that make your stories real and believable.

www.ingramcontent.com/pod-product-compliance
Lightning Source LLC
Chambersburg PA
CBHW060859280326
41934CB00007B/1114